BACK TO THE BEANSTALK

Enchantment and Reality for Couples

by

Judith R. Brown

Gestalt Institute of Cleveland Press
Cambridge, Massachusetts

Published by GICPress, Cambridge, Massachusetts
Gestalt Institute of Cleveland: 1517 Hazel Drive,
Cleveland, Ohio, 44106.

Distributed by The Analytic Press, Inc., Hillsdale, NJ.

Library of Congress Card No. 79-89476
ISBN 0-88163-295-3

Illustrations and cover art by Tonje Strøm
Layout and cover design by Arthur Roberts

ACKNOWLEDGMENTS FOR THE SECOND EDITION, 1998

To Nils Maganar Grendstad:

It was in the mid 1970's when I got the idea for using folktales to tackle the complex subject of relationships. A few years before, you had given me a book as a birthday gift. I have it before me now. You wrote: "Dec. 6. 1972. Judy, More than almost any book, this little one has helped me grow. And like the candle on the front cover you are shedding light and warmth around you, and on me. Thank you. And many happy returns of the day." You signed it, "With love, Nils." I have you in mind, Nils, as I write a new preface and the essay that will appear as an epilogue. Although I said goodbye to you for the last time over four years ago, you are still an inspiration for me, as well as for countless others. I have cherished your gift, Martin Buber's *The Way of Man: According to the Teaching of Hasidism.* It was this book that prompted the flash, the impulse, to use folktales for the rich material they contain about the nature of couples' relating. And imagine, all these years later, the fruits of your gift still come forth.

To Gordon Wheeler:

I have a fondness for this, my first book. You have lifted it from the background of my life and placed it on center stage, or more accurately, on my work table. In order to write the new preface and the epilogue I have had to read it through for the first time in about eighteen years. It seems like a grandchild: a great blessing that comes on the wings of someone else's efforts, yet it is mine. You are more like the parent who will shepherd it into the world. How grateful I am to you. I know you will prepare it well. How proud we both will be!

ACKNOWLEDGMENTS FOR THE FIRST EDITION, 1979

My great appreciation to Ted Berkman for his assistance. His expertise as writer and teacher was invaluable. To my friends, Genie Laborde who said, "Write it," and Chris Brainard for her constant faith and interest, I am especially grateful. Thanks to Jesse Thomas for his goodwill and editorial advice. And most important, thanks to my husband, George, for thirty years of matrimonial material, continued encouragement, and support.

**TO
GEORGE**

TABLE OF CONTENTS

FOREWORD

"Tell me a story"

To be human is to have a story, which grounds the self in itself, and also in time, place, purpose, and the world of other people. To be fully human is to be and feel a part of a larger story, a context of meaning and connection that is wider and deeper than the individual self as traditionally conceived, so that we can find ourselves outside ourselves in the world, as well as "inside"—and find that world inside us as well, as our world, the world we are responsible in and for. Every traditional culture knows this: indeed, "culture" itself is a story, which defines it and links its members to the whole, and the whole to the rest of the world. Without its story a society ceases to be a culture, a meaningful whole, and devolves instead into a cacophonous collection of warring parts, as we see around us everywhere in the world today. Every child knows it as well, because the experienced self is also a story, and the universal plea, "tell me a story," is always ultimately part of a quest for location and expansion of the self.

The Gestalt model knows this as well, for all that the articulation of narrative methods and concepts has lagged far behind many other terms of the model in its theoretical evolution. We recognize these truths not just in dream work and the dialogic or intersubjective encounter, for which Gestalt is justly well-known—but also in the most basic premises of phenomenology and the Gestalt field-organizational perspective themselves, both of which insist that "being in the world" is never a matter of just reacting to stimuli or "behavior," but always rests on and returns to the co-construction of meaningful wholes, which are the integration of the whole field of experience, the "inner world" of our memories, beliefs, needs, desires, and longings, together with the "outer world" of resources, dangers, origins and destinations—and most of all other people, who inhabit both domains. It is narrative which binds this whole experiential world together, and furnishes a place for us in it, and it in us, in the ongoing dynamic cocreation we experience as self-in-the-world.

Nearly a century ago now, the first generation of Gestaltists spoke of the properties of these wholes of meaning, which they called "good Gestalt," whose formation is our deepest nature and our nearly ceaseless activity. These properties were identified with terms like boundary, cohesion, distinction, vividness, articulation, brightness—and that most human of all qualities, which they called pregnance, the tendency of each situation, each meaningful whole, to go somewhere, to lead on to the next thing. This is the unfolding of our self-synergy, the impulse from within ourselves which joins with the energy of the larger field. "Pregnance" is also that directed self-organizational dimension we experience as purpose, which is both the legacy of our evolutionary psychology, and our most defining transcendent capacity. This is the "next" of Goodman's famous dictum, "here, now, next," that quality without which a story falls flat—and a life becomes empty, meaningless, "not worth living."

What has been less remarked is that these "good Gestalt" properties are exactly the characteristics of good story as well, as narrative therapists like Michael White and David Epston (1990) have discussed, using other language. This accounts for how it can be that a folk tale from China or Sumeria, perhaps from thousands of years ago, is immediately intelligible and entrancing to any child in Africa or the Americas today. Story is our deepest link to one another, as deep as embodiment itself; when we come to narrative, we arrive at a level of human nature that underlies and transcends culture and time, resting as it does on that most basic part of ourselves which creates both time and culture themselves, and then uses them as garments to dress our stories in. "Show me a culture where the people don't have names," says Gestalt teacher Sonia Nevis, "and I'll grant you that those people are too different from us, for there to be communication across cultural boundaries." We might go even further: show us a human group without stories, and we will question whether such a group is really human at all.

Meanwhile, as the Gestalt model has evolved and expanded in its perspectives and applications around the world, a whole separate tradition and school of narrative therapy has grown up, grounded in part in the family therapy movement, and receiving rich expression in the works of White & Epston (1990), Hoffman (1994) and Freedman & Combs (1996), to name just a few. The parallels and reverberations between these two approaches are both deep and resonant. Both are founded on the lived self-experience of the subjective person; each sees that subject as the active agent of self-organization in the field of experience; and both see the social construction of meaning as the central organizing activity of life, the process which organizes and informs behavior, growth, and relationship. It is time and past time for these two traditions to meet, enter into dialogue, and cross-fertilize each other in that energizing process we know in Gestalt as contact, the encounter which changes the organization of the shared field, thereby changing the co-participants in that field.

Thus it is important for Gestaltists to write about narrative, and the use of narrative in therapy, from a Gestalt point of view. This process has barely begun in the literature of Gestalt; yet as of this writing two significant volumes do already exist, both dealing in quite different ways with the creative interface between the two traditions, Gestalt and narrative therapy. One of these two is *The Collective Silence: German Families and the Legacy of Shame*, (Heimannsberg & Schmidt, 1994), in which a dozen German therapists, almost all of them trained in Gestalt, spin stories of their own lives and work with (and as) contemporary descendants of the World War II generation in Germany, as they and their clients struggle to mend a broken story, individually and collectively, and reclaim meaning and identity in their own lives—even when this reclaiming means the facing of tragic or unbearable truths, which have often been hidden away and screened with silence, by the families of victims, perpetrators, and bystanders alike. In the course of this work they all encounter together the universal lessons of healing and growth after unbearable trauma: namely, that tragedy and shame can never be borne and integrated alone; and that repair and restoration of self must begin with the telling and retelling of unbearable truth, over and over if necessary, to a willing and available listener, until that truth can be known, and shared, and reintegrated into a meaningful life narrative, for the individual and for the culture as a whole. For most of these writers, it was the Gestalt model which supported their return to the lived and felt terms of their own meaningful construction of self and context—which is to say, their stories—after long frustration and disappointment with some of their inherited therapy models, which seemed to dismiss their own need to create narrative meaning, in favor of imposed interpretation.

The other volume on this brief list is the one you now hold in your hand, the first to take up the use of story as a tool in an experiential approach informed by the principles of the Gestalt model. Here the well-known Gestalt teacher, writer, and therapist Judith Brown takes us on a magical excursion into the world of folklore and fairytale. There we find, as she says, people hilariously or uncomfortably like ourselves, as the case may be, in caricature or perhaps just more like some of our own worst moments, which many of us experience in the stuckness and repetitions that sometimes characterize couples' lives. The use of literature, Brown suggests, is to understand ourselves. The use of Gestalt, as she elaborates brilliantly in a reflective epilogue, is to enable us to ground that understanding in experiential, process terms—by which we mean the processes of contact, relationship, intimacy, and that cocreation of self and other which is synonymous with growth and healthy living.

That process of self-and-other understanding will never be more potentially instructive, more vivid on the page, and more just plain *fun*, than in the volume before you, which it is my great pleasure to introduce, and the publisher's great pride to reissue now, adding it to what we are confident will be a growing body of literature on the Gestalt uses of narrative, and the narrative uses of Gestalt. Read it and laugh with self-recognition; read it and weep, perhaps, for the same reason; most of all, read it and learn.

Gordon Wheeler
Cambridge Mass, 1998

PREFACE TO THE SECOND EDITION

Folktales have a remarkable endurance record. I delighted in them when they were read to me, I read them to my children and now I read them to my grandchildren. Isn't it amazing how we can identify with the characters in these timeless tales, see ourselves in their predicaments and interactions? During a particular incident, about twenty-two years ago, my own behavior reminded me of the ogre's wife in *Jack and the Beanstalk*. Thus came the idea to use couples in folktales as a springboard to discuss marriage relationships. (I use "marriage," to include adults in on-going intimate relationships, legal or not.) I wanted stories that reflect the absurdities of ordinary couples in their struggles to make a life together. In my work with couples, as well as in my own marriage, I am reminded over and over again that we often come to interactions we do not enjoy, interchanges that create distance when what we want is closeness, and we have not the remotest idea how we got there. We often know some of what our partner does, but we may not realize our own part in the drama.

These folktale couples do more than entertain us. Their exaggerated and repetitive behavior in relation to one another manifests what it truly means when we say "it takes two to tango." Their dances are easy to follow, step by step: the contrary wife and her husband, the spineless fisherman and his greedy wife, and the other hapless folktale characters in the following chapters. They go over the same ground, wearing deep ruts over the years, without a thought of changing what they do. How could they be expected to expand their restricted views and limited behaviors? Oh, and how like them we are! We limit our views of ourselves and our partner in narrow silhouettes and constrict our interactions to fit these cramped spaces.

If I were to write this book today it undoubtedly would be different. I am not the same twenty years later, nor is our world. Yet as I reread the book now I recognize and appreciate the simplicity and clarity of it. Although I touch on profound and complex questions of existence I avoid getting bogged down in philosophical discussions and theoretical explanations. (For those with an interest in theory and practice I include an epilogue.) The text is fresh and unspoiled and has been reported useful for couples on their own as well as for therapists using it with their clients.

The changeless character of the folktale world is unknown to us with our fast growing population and technological expansion, especially in the realm of information and communication. The many changes in our culture in the last years, from a proliferation of personal computers to the widespread use of Prozac, have had an impact on couples' relationships. Yet what partners need and want stays much the same, and this notwithstanding the dramatic change in the make-up of the majority couples. The traditional heterosexual, legally married couples are now outnumbered by pairs - of whatever gender or sexual preference - living together in committed relationships. In most couples, with or without children, both people are employed outside the home. One more tradition is thus left by the wayside: men bringing home the pay check while women take care of children, clean the house and keep the husband happy; or at least see that his clothes are clean and dinner is on the table. Couples' lives are further complicated by the by-products of divorce: ex-spouses, children from previous marriages, and blended, or step-families. These are all complex and can be difficult situations for both children and adults, intensifying the already tough job of creating a harmonious marriage.

The most basic need and desire as we become a couple seems to remain the same: sustaining a lasting bond with mutual love and support. Ideally we find joy with one another, that blessed state of ease and contentment which gives rise to the best in both of us. Because we are human we know sharing a life with another can be frustrating, painful, and just plain hard to do. Sometimes it seems like a matter of life and death to prove ourselves right! That is very human. But unlike the folktale couples, we can learn from experience, use our creativity, keep a sense of humor, and take that extra moment to see our partner, for we all need to be seen, really seen, and acknowledged.

Seeing ourselves is also essential. That is the main idea of using the stories, to gain more awareness of what we do in relation to our partner. One danger of seeing ourselves with more clarity is we are apt to do a very rapid two-step mental maneuver: become judgmental and tell ourselves we ought to make a plan for self-improvement. As an alternative I have included some questions and awareness exercises at the end of each chapter. I hope you will use them to discover more of you and more possibilities for the two of you. I hope they will provide shared and enjoyable, contactful experiences, leading to more lively choices and less automatic, repetitive, and boring interactions.

As human beings we are not perfect; probably not even perfectible. We get impatient, angry, petty, jealous, fearful, and infinitely hungry for love. We are often divided, in conflict within ourselves. We think thoughts we tell ourselves we must not think; we feel emotions we judge wrong or inappropriate. We utter words that we do not intend. We have unrealistic expectations - for ourselves and those we marry. It is good to remind ourselves sometimes to come from a place of love, from the only place where what we see as our beloved's imperfections are not used to build a case against him or her, but seen and appreciated as signs of their humanness: their fears and longings that mirror our own.

PREFACE TO THE FIRST EDITION

Looking into a fun house mirror, no matter how distorted our image, we can still recognize ourselves. In fact, artists have taught us that exaggeration and distortion can help us discover reality. In this collection, I hold up several folktale marriages as magnifying glasses that may, through the exaggeration that is intrinsic in folktales, help us to recognize ourselves and our own behavior in our marriages.

The word "marriage" is used to include all intimate, ongoing relationships between adults. "Husband" and "wife" are used for the sake of convenience, but they can refer to a partner of either sex.

Just as the reflection in a distorted glass is not an accurate picture of ourselves, so these folktale characters are not intended as true life representations, but rather as heightened examples of behavior that, in varying degrees and in various situations, we all know from our experiences.

Folktales have nourished our dreams and provided our romantic fantasies about marriage. We have all been fed, along with our mothers' milk, such make-believe as, "some day my prince will come," and "they lived happily ever after." Now let's look at the folktales on another level, as reflections of reality. Perhaps with their help we can relinquish our outrageous expectations of ourselves and our partners and learn new ways of being truly engaged with another. With new awareness and some effort, our dreams of a rich, satisfying life in marriage may some day come true.

Note: No slight intended. For convenience the male pronoun has generally been used in this work.

CHAPTER I

TWO IN A SIEVE

They went to sea in a sieve, they did;
  In a sieve they went to sea:
In spite of all their friends could say,
On a winter's morn, on a stormy day,
  In a sieve they went to sea.
And when the sieve turned round and round,
And everyone cried, "You'll all be drowned!"
They called aloud, "Our sieve ain't big;
But we don't care a button, we don't care a fig:
  In a sieve we'll go to sea!"

From "The Jumblies" by Edward Lear

Getting married, for many of us, is a good deal like going to sea in a sieve. Like the Jumblies, we have meager equipment and an uncertain future, but that does not stop us. Whatever impelled the Jumblies to set out on their risky voyage, they were helped along by their high hopes. And so are we. A wedding is a delightful beginning, a starting point, when in our happy imaginations all dreams are still realizable. Like the Jumblies, we know we are going to make it!

1

What high hopes launch *us* into marriage? The list is long and varied, sensible and ridiculous, spoken and unspoken, possible and impossible to attain. Underneath everything is the hope of sharing our life with someone special, of touching and being touched intimately by another. That hope motivates us to take the big step. That cherished dream keeps us paddling and bailing, even when the going gets rough.

For although we imagine our marriage will be like a beautiful, sturdy yacht skimming along a calm sea, it turns out to be a craft that is scarcely seaworthy. Soon it is springing leaks. The seams labelled "money," "sex," "power," "in-laws," and "children," are threatening to go. To make things worse, as we look around us, the boats of friends and relatives are foundering. It seems that if anything is to be done about our situation we'll have to do it ourselves. But we don't know what to do. Dreams, buttressed by determination, may temporarily keep us from sinking, but to keep afloat is not enough. Who wants to struggle all the time? We want to feel good—soak up some sunshine, take in some scenery and enjoy the trip. What's holding us back?

First, there are the immediate difficulties of being plunged into a new and intimate relationship: the need to mesh two lives, two sets of attitudes and habits, is incredibly demanding. It requires the talents of an international negotiator, the sensitivity of a brain surgeon, the endurance of a long distance runner, not to mention faith, intelligence, and a sense of humor. We may find ourselves short in those attributes. Equally disheartening, we usually find that we are stuck with old habits that don't serve us well at all.

As if these problems aren't enough, we compound them with three persistent hazards: our impossible notions of how marriage "should" be; our ever-present fears; and our lack

2

of experience and equipment (what, no oars?).

Even before the nuptials we are bombarded with unreasonable standards for an "ideal marriage," and to some degree we accept them as our goals. We think, "Yes, that's right. My marriage *should* be creative, full of joy, open and honest; I *should* be loving, spontaneous, and growing." These words have great power and little clarity. They entrap us in a net of "shoulds" and persuade us that we ought to live up to someone else's vague expectations. If we try to fulfill these pie-in-the-sky hopes we are doomed to failure and disappointment.

The second hazard is fear. Fear is apparently unknown to the Jumblies. They "don't care a fig" for the winter storm or the warnings of their friends. Unfortunately, the rest of us are not so immune. As *we* set off in marriage, our fears march at our sides. We not only take along the nightmares of our past but we invent the possible tragedies of the future. We are terrified that our partners may leave us. We will be left alone. No one will love us. Fear drives us to manipulations and power struggles. Fear pushes us together and pulls us apart.

The third hazard is our inexperience. We don't automatically know how to be married; we have few tools for coping with our new situation. Being with someone special brings joy and contentment, but when our reality falls short of our unrealistic expectations it also brings dissatisfaction, discouragement, loneliness, and hostility. How do we get stuck this way? How can we avoid it?

Two of the surest and quickest ways to get stuck are "defending" and "blaming." Disagreements are inevitable. When some unpleasantness develops in our relationship or there's an argument, we assume that only one person is at fault, and of course, it's the *other* person. So we blame:

"It's your fault because you're so bitchy."
"If you wouldn't be like that, everything would be fine."
"You never listen to me."
"You always want to be right."

Or we shift into reverse: instead of blaming the other person, we defend ourselves.

"It's not *my* fault. I was really trying."
"I was only doing what you told me."
"Yes, but what I did wasn't as bad as what *you* did."

This last example actually combines both defending *and* blaming. It's not long before we become at least dimly aware that these tactics aren't getting us anywhere. They may even be hurtful to our partners and our relationship. But we are carried away again and again by our desire to prove our innocence and to deny that any change is required on *our* part.

Defending and blaming are not the only ways to get stuck. Our inexperience can also take us into other traps. An invaluable aid in avoiding them and creating a successful relationship is to develop an awareness of ourselves: our feelings, our emotions, and our thoughts. Often we know how we *should* feel ("I'm in bed with my husband, I *should* feel love and desire"), what we *should* want ("I *should* want my wife to be successful and to be promoted"), and what it is *right* to think ("It's right to think he's doing this for both of us") without knowing what we actually *do* feel, want, and think.

"Knowing thyself" can be understood more easily by looking at children than by listening to philosophers. How do children know when they are hungry? By the clock? No, by the stomach. How do they know when they are frustrated, cold, angry, frightened, or satisfied? They know directly by

4

how they *feel;* from their experience of themselves in the moment. And they communicate their state readily and directly. As adults we have learned so many clever ways to avoid our experience of the moment that our bodies transmit messages in vain. We are left with a minimum of authentic experience and response. The radio in our heads persists in broadcasting words, but it is not plugged in to the scene of action.

Obviously, being married doesn't feel so good as long as we are stuck. The problem is, too often we can't see the difficulty. It is concealed, veiled, elusive; we may not even be aware that it exists. And yet, although no two marriages are identical and no one formula can resolve all issues, there *are* ways to tackle the obstacles, both real and imaginary, that bedevil our marital journey. To escape the coils we wind around each other we must *perceive* what we are doing, *experience* what we are feeling, and *communicate* with each other—in ways that may seem strange at first. For instance with the familiar defending and blaming:

"You're impossible to talk to."
"You always misinterpret what I say."
"It would kill you to say you're sorry."

Hear the difference when feelings are expressed:

She: "I'm feeling disappointed this afternoon."
He: "I was wondering what was eating you. I have a feeling of 'watch out—here it comes'."
She: (Laughing) "Ya. I guess I was ready to blast you."

Still there may be an argument, but in the above exchange there is contact, there is listening, authenticity, awareness of and expression of feelings and emotions. These people start their sentences with "I." We all have emotions and the capacity to express them. As we increase our ability to respond from our emotions, we enrich our opportunities to share how we are. As we share how we are, we add to our ability to respond from our emotions. Then we come alive. Vitality and excitement embellish us; we become three-dimensional, better acquainted with ourselves and each other.

With this approach we can ride past the traditional hazards that impede our course; armed with alternatives of perceiving, experiencing and communicating, we can throw away the yardstick that nobody could possibly measure up to, develop new tools that enable us to relate in different ways. We can even share our fears.

A marriage does not just happen to us. We are not simply swept along in a sieve through an ever-changing sea. We are the builders of our marriage boat, the authors of our lives together. As authors we write our scripts, choose the parts we play, and create our own folktales.

The folktale couples you'll meet in the pages to come are not all as likable and engaging as the Jumblies. Some will strike you as strange, irritating, or even mildly shocking. But they all have something to tell us. The spotlight that we cast on their marriages can help us illuminate our own.

And the Jumblies, as a later verse informs us, did return safely from their hazardous trip to a "beautiful dumpling feast."

And in twenty years they all came back,—
  In twenty years or more:
And everyone said, "How tall you've grown! . . ."

INTRODUCTION TO "QUESTIONS" AND
"AWARENESS EXPERIENCES"

Following each chapter are two sections titled "Questions" and "Awareness Experiences." Some readers may wish to skip these sections, at least for now, and go on with the reading of the book. Others, however, may wish to do one or both of the sections as they read. There is no obligation in either case. It all depends on the reader's needs.

The "Questions" are suggested for individual readers who would like to relate what they are reading more directly to their own experience. The questions are open-ended: they are meant to help highlight and clarify experience. There are no "right" or "wrong" answers. They are for the sake of *describing*, not evaluating or judging. They can be done with or without the others person present. If the other person *is* present and either person finds himself judging or being judged, simply share your awareness and move on.

The "Awareness Experiences" require that both people be present. They are suggested for couples who would like more contact with themselves and each other, who are willing to experiment with new ways of interacting. In our culture we have come to look for "immediate relief" for any condition that doesn't feel good to us. These experiences are not "magic cures," nor is growth instantaneous. With time and practice, however, it is possible to get in touch with ourselves and others, and, just as important, to become aware of how we interfere and interrupt our getting in touch.

QUESTIONS FOR CHAPTER I

1. Did you go into your relationship with high hopes? Which of these now seem unrealistic?

2. If you could tell a young couple just starting out one thing they should know, what would that be?

3. Are there any fears that you brought with you to your marriage that you can laugh at now?

AWARENESS EXPERIENCES FOR CHAPTER I

Read through the exercises. If either partner has any objection to doing the exercises, or any part of them, talk about these objections. Be aware of the quality of communication. Is it without defending and blaming?

1. Sit facing each other. Do not touch. Close your eyes. Take a minute to pay attention to yourself.

2. Now open your eyes and look at each other. Don't talk yet. Take a minute to look. As you do this, experience how you feel. (CAUTION: Experiencing how you feel is *not* interpretation or analysis of yourself or your partner. It is being aware of your physical sensations: breathing, muscle tensions, body temperature, etc.)

3. Now close your eyes. How is it for you with your eyes closed now? Do you feel relieved? Cut off? At peace? Other?

4. After a couple of minutes open your eyes and make contact by looking *and* by touching hands. No talking yet. Do this for at least two minutes.

5. Close your eyes and break hand contact. Again experience how you are.

6. Open your eyes and talk about this experience. What did you like about it? What did you not like about it? What surprised you?

The following may be done separately or discussed together.

9

AWARENESS QUESTIONS:

What got in the way of your *seeing* your partner? Were you *evaluating* as you were looking? (He should shave every day. Or, her hair needs washing.)

Were you busy worrying or wondering what your partner was seeing while looking at you?

Were you talking to yourself?

Were you "trying" to do it right?

These and many other mental activities can get in the way of perceiving and experiencing.

Could you feel the other's hands? How do you know when your hands are in contact? Pressure? Temperature? Other?

When you talked about your experience, did you censor your comments? On what basis? Were you afraid of sounding foolish? Were you afraid of hurting your partner's feelings?

It takes time to learn from exercises such as these. It is suggested that you set aside a few minutes every day to do them.

CHAPTER II

THE OGRE AND HIS WIFE

Jack the giant killer is well known to every child. Sent to market to sell a cow, his mother's last possession, he makes a seemingly poor exchange; he swaps the cow for a handful of brightly colored beans. His mother, as you might expect, is not as intrigued as Jack is by the beans. She berates Jack for his foolishness and angrily throws the beans out of the window. The discarded beans grow magically overnight.

The beanstalk grew up quite close past Jack's window; so all he had to do was to open it and give a jump on to the beanstalk which ran up just like a big ladder. So Jack climbed, and he climbed, and he climbed, and he climbed, and he climbed, and he climbed, and he climbed till at last he reached the sky. And when he got there he found a long broad road going as straight as a dart. So he walked along, and he walked along, and he walked along till he came to a great big tall house, and on the doorstep there was a great big tall woman.

"Good morning, mum," says Jack, quite polite-like. "Could you be so kind as to give me some breakfast?" For he hadn't had anything to eat, you know, the night before, and was as hungry as a hunter.

11

"It's breakfast you want, is it?" says the great big tall woman. "It's breakfast you'll be if you don't move off from here. My man is an ogre and there's nothing he likes better than boys broiled on toast. You'd better be moving on or he'll soon be coming."

"Oh! please mum, do give me something to eat, mum. I've had nothing to eat since yesterday morning, really and truly, mum," says Jack. "I may as well be broiled as die of hunger."

Well, the ogre's wife was not half so bad after all. So she took Jack into the kitchen and gave him a chunk of bread and cheese and a jug of milk. But Jack hadn't half finished these when thump! thump! thump! the whole house began to tremble with the noise of someone coming.

"Goodness gracious me! It's my old man," said the ogre's wife, "What on earth shall I do? Come along quick and jump in here." And she bundled Jack into the oven just as the ogre came in.

He was a big one, to be sure. At his belt he had three calves strung up by the heels, and he unhooked them and threw them down on the table and said: "Here, wife, broil me a couple of these for breakfast. Ah! what's that I smell?

Fee-fi-fo-fum
I smell the blood of an Englishman,
Be he alive, or be he dead
I'll have his bones to grind my bread."

"Nonsense, dear," said his wife, "you're dreaming. Or perhaps you smell the scraps of that little boy you liked so much for yesterday's dinner. Here you go and have a wash and tidy up, and by the time you come back your breakfast'll be ready for you."

So off the ogre went, and Jack was just going to jump out of the oven and run away when the woman told him not

12

to. "Wait till he's asleep," says she; "he always has a doze after breakfast."

Well, the ogre had his breakfast, and after that he goes to a big chest and takes out of it a couple of bags of gold, and down he sits and counts till at last his head began to nod, and he began to snore till the whole house shook again.

Then Jack crept out on tiptoe from his oven, and as he was passing the ogre he took one of the bags of gold under his arm, and off he pelters till he came to the beanstalk, and then he threw down the bag of gold, which of course fell into his mother's garden, and then he climbed down, and climbed down, till at last he got home . . .

Jack worms his way into the giant's house a second time and makes off with a hen that lays golden eggs. On his third trip to the land above the clouds, Jack gets hold of the giant's golden harp but it almost costs him his life. In a suspenseful moment he races back to the beanstalk with the giant close on his heels. Down the beanstalk in a flash to his mother's garden goes Jack, and with an axe he chops down the beanstalk, giant and all. Jack has redeemed himself; he and his mother are never in need again.

Jack's adventures make exciting reading for children, but is there another story here, a hidden story that has something to say to adults? What about the ogre and his wife?

The ogre in this folktale is a tyrannical husband. He rules the roost—or so it seems. A man of few words, when he speaks he either shouts orders: "Wife, broil me a couple of these for breakfast," or he roars his threats: "Fee-fi-fo-fum . . ." With his enormous body and his booming voice he bullies his way around. However, like all bullies, he is a child at the core. He even has toys to play with. He takes

13

out his gold to count after breakfast; he coaxes his hen to lay golden eggs and persuades his harp to sing. These are his playthings. This giant bully has more brawn than brains.

His wife knows this; it gives her the clue as to how to handle him. Terrified she may be of his formidable size and his threats, but she knows that underneath he's a little boy. Like a child he is easily duped; he is quickly soothed by her tranquil words when he "smells the blood of an Englishman." She is alert to his moods and attentive to his demands. Determined to keep peace in the family by any means, she dutifully plays the submissive wife, thereby avoiding a direct confrontation.

However, her true power is that of the saboteur. She sneaks Jack into the house, feeds and protects him—then flatly denies that he's there. She undermines the ogre even more subtly by the manner in which she speaks to him: not as a wife to her husband but more as mother to child. Her ultimate act of sabotage occurs when the ogre goes off to wash. Although Jack could then take the opportunity to escape, Mrs. Ogre insists that he remain in the oven. It is from this vantage point that he finds out about the ogre's gold, which soon after, of course, becomes Jack's gold. The ogre's wife, with conscious intent or not, is Jack's accomplice and largely responsible for her husband's downfall.

So these are the folks who live upstairs! Together they make quite a pair. At first glance we see a top-dog husband and an under-dog wife. When he demands his meal, she prepares it. When he fee-fi-fo-fums, she assures him that all is well: "Nonsense, dear, you're dreaming." We can even imagine her tone of voice, pseudo-sympathetic, warm and motherly. "Here, you go wash now and tidy up."

But what is the effect on her husband? He is pacified for

14

the moment, to be sure, and yet he is somehow diminished. Over a period of time these tactics leave him chronically frustrated and confused. Just what is happening? He may well wonder! He *knows* he smells the blood of an Englishman. He fee-fi-fo-fums around the house. His fury builds. And each time his wife lulls him with, "Nonsense, dear, you're dreaming." She thoroughly ignores his experience and his feelings about his experience. She takes the wind out of his sails; he is disarmed. He may finally say to himself, "I guess she's right. I *don't* smell an Englishman." He is a blustering bully or a pacified child, but never do we see him stand up to his wife as a man.

The giant's frustration and confusion are easy to trace. When his wife is not quieting him, she apparently exerts herself to comply with his every bidding. Nonetheless, he is constantly left with a vague, irksome feeling that she is never really *with* him, that she doesn't support him, but rather that he is waging some kind of annoying battle that is never openly declared, never fought and finished up.

An added frustration for the ogre is the fact that his wife, to all appearances, is completely blameless. Of course *we* know that she is responsible for allowing Jack into the house, feeding him, and protecting him from the ogre, *but* (under-dog always has a "but") she is surely doing a good, kind, and noble deed to care for the lad. So, in the ogre's muddled head, how can she be censured for that? And when his wife is good, kind, and noble, the husband is surely an ogre if he doesn't appreciate her virtue. The ogre's gnawing irritation fans the flames of his tyrannical behavior. His vexation accumulates; like the Chinese water torture, it wears away at him. He doesn't know how to handle this situation. He could say to his wife, "Look here, you're irritating me."

That would be one way to handle it; but with his lack of awareness it doesn't occur to him. So his irritation grows, and he blows. When he blows, she shushes.

Meanwhile Mrs. Ogre silently suffers her own frustration. Her martyred existence brings her little satisfaction. Bored and discontented, she stockpiles her resentments. It's all *his* fault that she has to sneak the young man in behind his back. If he were not such an unreasonable ogre, she could openly invite Jack in, and there would be no problem. They might even enjoy the guest together! The one thing she will not do is assert herself directly, or become her own person. Her energy is expended either in spiting her husband's demands or slavishly complying, in defending herself against his angry attacks or pleasing him.

Both of these characters have a limited repertoire. Like actors going through the same scene over and over, they know unconsciously all the lines and gestures. They play their roles to perfection, firmly settled into mutual patterns of manipulation and control that are predictable, constant, and unchanging. Do you imagine that this is the first time the ogre's wife has hushed him with, "Nonsense, dear," when her husband has come bellowing into the house? Nor is it the last. The scene is repeated when Jack returns. Repetition brings no surprises and little pleasure; in fact it gets boring. The ogre and his wife always know what to expect. Like many other couples they rely on habitual, rigid, programmed ways to live out their time together.

What does it do for the beanstalk couple, or for you and me, to stay as we are? What do our mutual contracts and control do for us? Whatever our reciprocal patterns may be, they keep us safe on familiar territory. Let's face it; when today is just like yesterday and tomorrow again the same, you don't have to exert yourself. A lazy switch to automatic pilot is the only effort required. Each situation that arises is ground that has been covered.

As long as the ogre's wife apparently complies with her husband's demands, life will proceed in its usual routine. The ogre will vaguely experience his frustration, will explode frequently in anger, demand that his wishes be met, and continue along this familiar, well-traveled road he knows so well. His wife will have her soothing words for herself and her husband. She will add excitement to her dull existence by allowing or creating manageable, explosive situations for which she will take no responsibility. She will remain secure in her good, semi-martyr role, always being in the right. Like the ogre and his wife, you and I tend to stick with what we know. The unexpected creates tremors for us; the familiar feels safe. And safety is something very precious to us. Because on the other side of safety lies fear.

And we are so afraid. Although we keep our fears well hidden from our partners and sometimes even from ourselves, they have a powerful influence on our relationships. It is our fears, our dim panic at the thought of being exposed to a threatening unknown—that keep us clinging desperately to what we know—games of manipulation and control. We want intensely to be connected with at least one other person intimately, in a positive and significant way. And yet, at the same time, we are so afraid of losing in the process something of ourselves. As great as our craving may be to alleviate our essential aloneness, we feel so vulnerable, so exposed when we open ourselves to another.

Like the ogre and his wife, we settle for partnership roles that link us together, but together in a way that keeps us empty and wanting more. We maintain a firm hold on our

17

mate while at the same time we remain hidden and apart, out of contact with each other. We maintain a precarious balance, a kind of tightrope existence, on the one hand holding fast to our own personality and individuality, and on the other being joined together with another person.

Through our games we remain impervious to both our own nature and that of our partner. We get into the habit of ducking behind our roles. We believe that to reveal ourselves is to get hurt, to give ourselves away and lose some advantage over our partner. This leads us into one of the saddest and most absurd of fantasies: we imagine that if anyone really knew us, he would find us lacking. What a dilemma we find ourselves in! Like the ogre and his wife we are caught in a rut.

Is there any way out? Do we really want to get out? Can we give up our safety, leave our familiar ground, abandon the old set of rules and set off with our partner on an adventure? The ogre and his wife and all the rest of us have developed habits that have served us for a long time. Letting go of the old patterns is hard work, a long and difficult and sometimes exciting struggle. It's like growing up, and that isn't easy at any age.

The first step in transforming a relationship is to reach the awareness that all is not well. The ogre and his wife never come to that point. They never take the opportunity to say to one another how they are feeling about themselves, their marriage, or each other. We now know that it matters how we feel, and it is important to talk about what's going on with us. Also important is to know our partner. How lonely and sad to look at your marriage partner after twenty years and think to yourself, "I don't know anything about this person." Marriage is not a poker game, to be played behind a facade of bluff and indifference. Can you genuinely love and care about your partner without knowing him? Or enhance his life when you can't make contact, when you don't know who he is and what is taking place on his inner stage? Since we are not robots—fixed and undeviating—but rather feeling, acting, and reacting people, it is essential that we keep in touch with one another, that we look and see, listen and hear.

The main point is that we *pay attention* to what is going on, with ourselves and our partners. This sounds easy but in fact is a difficult thing to do, for we tend to see and hear what we *want* to have happening rather than what is happening. When it comes to getting in touch with our own power games and manipulations we find it is close to impossible without the help of another. Yet if that other should be our partner, we are not likely to be receptive. We feel blamed and want to defend. And partners are often as confused as we ourselves, for the interaction between couples is complex.

There is always so much going on. Take for example the wifely ultimatum: "If you leave me, I'll kill myself." First, there is the context in which this is spoken. Let's imagine a husband packing a suitcase, a determined look on his face, angry shouts still echoing in the bedroom. Second, there are the words themselves. Third, there is the emotion with which the words are spoken. Fourth, there is the history of these two people, their history together as well as separately, what they know about each other and what they imagine. Complicated? You bet it is. And the husband's response will reflect what *he* hears, what *he* sees, what *he* feels, what *he* knows, and what *he* imagines. There is little chance that he can tell his wife at that moment that she is manipulating him openly, powerfully, and perhaps effectively, and less chance that she will hear him. And the wife, whose deepest fear is that she will be abandoned, is in no position to tell her husband that she experiences his leaving as a manipulation.

We want to pay attention and keep in touch, but where do we look? On which level do we listen? At a three ring circus you're bound to miss something. It's impossible to pay attention to everything at the same time. So it is between couples. If in our attempts to keep in touch with our partners we stick just to the debating level or to the shouts and threats, we'll miss the *real* action. Let's listen to what the wife in our example might say if she spoke at another level, or what her husband might hear if he would listen through to what lies beyond the original words: "When you threaten to leave, I'm terrified. I'll do anything to make you stay. I'll blackmail you into staying." Or she might say, "Everyone I've ever cared for has left me and I knew you would, too. If you leave I'll know I'm no good. There'll be nothing for me. It'll all be your fault. I see no choice and I'm scared." Here we are getting to the real action. The wife discloses to her husband how she feels. Something else is happening, too. She is also acknowledging what's going on with her, letting herself feel her emotions. At that moment she is completely paying attention. This is the second step necessary to get out of the rut of manipulations and power struggles. First we become aware that all is not going well; we lift our heads out of the sand. Then we pay attention to what we are doing and how we are doing it: what we are experiencing, and how we can express it.

The instant we pay attention to what *is*, the *is* itself changes. That may sound like a bit of folktale magic but it is not. Growth and change do not occur mystically, or "once upon a time." They are the outcome and the result of the process

20

of living, of on-going experience. The *recognition* of what we are doing and the *awareness* of our feelings and actions raise the curtain on a new scene where we have many choices.

Choices are precisely what the ogre and his wife do not have. They are stuck in a rut, and have neither the will nor the imagination to get out of it. Onto the deeply-worn grooves of this stage happens unsuspecting Jack. Like a child coming into a family, he is immediately drawn into the relationship of the couple. The wife uses him to bring some excitement into her life and get at her husband. The husband uses him to vent his anger and frustration.

When the ogre's wife agrees to give food and protection to Jack, she behaves as if she has no choices. The fact is, she has many alternatives. Since she is much bigger than he is and need not be threatened by him, she could choose to not give him food. Or she could invite him in, feed him, then roast him as she has done others to give her husband a treat. Conversely, she could assert herself and demand her right to do as she chooses, without threats and recriminations from her husband.

Instead, she goes into her robot-like act of subtle defiance. First she feeds the young man; then, to aggravate the situation, she suggests that Jack hide in the oven. From this location Jack can see the ogre counting his gold, can see when the ogre drops off to sleep, and is able to take full advantage of the situation. The wife's program to sabotage her husband has taken over and she does a superb job of it. The ogre becomes her victim. She remains blameless, takes no responsibility for her actions, and escapes becoming the direct object of her husband's rage.

Are there alternatives for the ogre as well as for his wife? There are *always* alternatives, once we dare to step out of

21

our old roles. The ogre could look at his wife as he walks in the door.

"Well, wife, you're looking fine this morning; will you join me for brunch?" Or he might even call her by her name.

"Mathilda, watch out, I'm on the warpath this morning. Don't mess with me." Or:

"What's going on here? I'm sniffing something and I'd say that something is an Englishman!" And when she pooh-poohs his suspicions and tells him to wash up for breakfast:

"Wife, when I say I'm smelling something, and you tell me it's nonsense, you make me mighty furious."

Which might provoke a quite different response:

"Well, I *do* have a surprise for you. Just look in the oven." You see, there are so many possibilities now. When the hero or the heroine changes, the plot cannot remain the same.

Openness and exchange do not guarantee instant resolution of all conflicts, nor solution of all problems. But they are the indispensable beginning. What is important between two people is the process, the process of dialogue, of communication: the expression of good will and caring. When a couple makes the commitment to see and hear what is going on between them, to experience and be aware of themselves and their partners, then the process has begun.

QUESTIONS FOR CHAPTER II

1. Do the Ogre and his wife remind you of anyone you know?

2. Are there times when *you* are like the ogre? Like his wife?

3. Is there any sabotage going on in your relationship?

4. As you read this chapter, were you taking sides? What does that tell you about you? Can you imagine taking the other side? Do you have something to say for the other side?

AWARENESS EXPERIENCES FOR CHAPTER II

Read through the exercises. Share with each other your attitude toward doing them. Be aware of judgments of yourself and the other as you discuss this. Do you consider one attitude to be "better" than another? Do your judgments get in the way of your listening to one another? Do you avoid defending and blaming?

In this exercise you will take turns. Decide now who will go first.

Sit opposite each other. Do not touch. No. 1 will make two concise statements. No. 2 will simply listen. No response is required.

No. 1 will tell No. 2 one thing that he *sees* as he looks at 2: "I see . . ." and finish the sentence. Examples: I see you looking at me. Or, I see your mouth open. Or, I see you looking down. Then No. 1 will tell what he *imagines* when he looks at No. 2. "I imagine . . ." Examples: I imagine you are curious. Or, I imagine you are bored. Or, I imagine you are sad.

Now No. 2 will take a turn and make two concise statements. The first begins with, "I see . . ." and the second with, "I imagine . . ."

Each person takes several turns. Talk about this experience. How did you feel doing it? How do you feel now? What surprised you?

Now do the exercise again. Let the person who went second last time go first this time. Now add a third sentence. After "I see . . ." "I imagine . . ." add "I am . . ." Examples: I am amused, or I am feeling serious, or I am feeling excited. The person who is doing the exercise *responds* to what he sees and what he imagines. Each takes several turns. Again, talk about the experience.

AWARENESS QUESTIONS:

How did you decide who would go first? Is this typical of the way you come to decisions? As you discuss this, do you blame and defend? Can you discuss this without blaming and defending?

When you talked about the experience, did you have enough time to express yourself? Did you feel listened to and understood by your partner?

Would you like your partner to talk more? Less? What would this do for you?

During the exercise were you evaluating how well you and/or your partner were doing?

Judging, evaluating, and comparing are all ways to interfere with perceiving, experiencing, and communicating.

CHAPTER III

TITTY MOUSE AND TATTY MOUSE

Titty Mouse lived in a house and Tatty Mouse lived in a house. So they both lived in a house.

Titty Mouse had porridge for breakfast and Tatty Mouse had porridge for breakfast. So they both had porridge for breakfast.

Titty Mouse went to market and Tatty Mouse went to market. So they both went to market.

Titty Mouse planted corn and Tatty Mouse planted corn. So they both planted corn.

What boredom! What banal monotony! There is no vitality, no force, no emotion in this dull marriage. Two disconnected beings yoked together living side by side. They may not argue much but they don't laugh a lot, either.

Chances are that Titty Mouse and Tatty Mouse didn't start out as mirror reflections of each other. Even among mice there are differences: there's the city mouse and the country mouse, the timid mouse and the daring mouse, the homeloving mouse and the mouse who wants to see the world.

In fact, it's frequently the differences that draw couples

together. If you've got a plus for my minus, then you're the one for me. My emptiness reaches out for your fullness. The ways we are unlike may or may not be apparent; when we choose our mate we seem to have a sixth sense for ferreting out qualities or attitudes that contrast with our own. Take Bert, whose greatest pleasure is to closet himself in his workshop; he marries Gladys who is an absolute whirlwind of activity. Tom runs marathons every chance he gets while Susan, his wife, lounges in the hammock with a cookbook and a box of chocolates. Florence smiles bravely through life, swallowing all resentments; her partner is Richard, whose rage erupts with volcanic regularity. They have all found someone with something they haven't. As we all discover in our relationships, our differences can kindle interest and excitement.

Excitement and vitality, painfully absent in the Titty and Tatty Mouse marriage, vibrate through the union that has room for differences. A life-giving tension results. For some of us, tension has become a dirty word; we have come to believe it's something we don't want, an aggravating state, the opposite of pleasure. But tension is as necessary in a marriage as in a work of art; without it a partnership becomes stagnant and flat. The presence of a second person, a separate individual with whom we can interact, share, and learn adds variety and energy.

Another kind of excitement comes from the joy of discovering that we have married someone whose talents mesh with our own inadequacies: someone who loves to cook up specialties for guests or who nimbly computes the income tax, or fills the house with beautiful music. Like Jack Sprat and his wife, together you can lick the platter clean. Even Bert in his workshop doesn't want to cut himself off completely from

27

the world; yet this is what would happen if Gladys didn't keep in touch with family and friends. And Tom, home from the marathon and relaxing after a shower, relishes Susan's latest gastronomical experiment. Interdependence makes life fuller. Each partner contributes to the total picture; neither has to be sufficient in all things.

Differences in interests and talents can be unexpectedly enriching; but as we all find out sooner or later, there are other kinds of differences—in attitudes, habits and self-expression—that can cause trouble.

When a couple takes up life together they may hardly be aware of the less obvious differences between them, the ones that may not show immediately, or be temporarily hidden by the first rush of being in love. Contact and time bring these to the surface, then magnify them. Take the case of Bob and Jan. They began their marriage like two people poised comfortably near the mid-point of a seesaw. After a while they found themselves arguing about something they had assumed they saw eye to eye on; how often they should get together with their parents. Bob wanted to have less and less to do with them. "Let's skip the visit this weekend."

As he shifted backward from the mid-point, Jan countered by resisting. Then as Bob became more adamant she began moving in the other direction, demanding more contact with the parents. Communication became difficult, if not impossible, as each fought to convince the other to give a little. Neither was willing. The distance grew between the two; each tended to dig in and hold his position. They ended at opposite extremes. When couples find themselves at extremes it's easy then to give up trying to reach each other; they slip quietly into a Titty Mouse, Tatty Mouse union.

This same pattern is repeated in many aspects of a relationship. Here are some examples you may have encountered. As Joan gets more strict with the children, Don gets more lenient, which in turn pushes Joan toward a more emphatic stand. In another case, the more Doris says, "I don't care which movie we go to," the more Al takes over the decisions—not only about movies but about which furniture to buy and what to eat for dinner. Then passive Doris becomes even more passive. John wears rose-colored glasses and assures Helen that everything is going to be fine; meanwhile, Helen's worry lines grow deeper. Barbara's emotions intensify; Harold becomes more calm and logical. Each is pushed closer to the end of the seesaw by the backward step of the other. They are about to fall off the edge; what started as a dream has turned into a nightmare.

Sometimes the very qualities that drew us to our partner when extended in other directions or expressed in other ways become irksome, and finally intolerable; what was initially a charming idiosyncrasy becomes with time a thorn in our side. We ask ourselves, "What did I see in this person, anyway?" Yet, it is really not so mysterious that we latch onto someone with tendencies that we both love and hate, with characteristics that we want and don't want. It is those facets of personality that give us trouble in ourselves which also trouble us in our partners. What we run away from in ourselves we embrace in the other—but only for a while. Then we fight with them as we have fought with ourselves.

Bob, the young man on the seesaw, really doesn't know what to do about his mother and father. He has mixed feelings. He is actually going through an argument with himself along these lines:

"Hey, Bob, what's with you? Your folks have done a lot for you. You really should call them."

He gives himself a quick comeback. "Yeah, but you open the door to them, and they want to take over your life. They never get off your back. I don't want anything to do with them."

Meanwhile, Jan, his wife, has been wrestling with a similar internal tug of war. She, however, reaches the opposite conclusion—that they *should* call the parents. She says aloud, "Let's invite your folks and mine to dinner." Bob's immediate reply coming directly out of his conversation with himself is, "I don't want anything to do with any of them." She says, "But they're our parents! Look at all they've done for us!"

From that point on he doesn't have to be his own adversary. His wife has walked right into that role, and the battle is no longer between Bob and Bob. It is now waged between Bob and Jan. The firmer her position, the deeper he digs in. Who can win?

When polarities develop like this, partners all but lose sight of each other. Yet the longing for closeness and harmony persists. In desperation each tends to blame the other for the distance. "Everything would be fine if you thought like me," or ". . . felt like me," or ". . . *were* like me." "If you were like me all our troubles would be over." The attitude is summed up by Henry Higgins in *My Fair Lady*, "Why can't a woman be like a man?"

Generally this demand is not stated directly but is clearly implied. One partner asks, "How can you get so impatient with me when you did the same thing last week and I didn't say a word?" The message is, "You should be like me." Or, "How can you spend so much money on foolish things. *I* only buy what I need." Again the same message, "You should be like me."

Out of fear, for the sake of peace and quiet, or for any number of possible reasons, one partner may surrender. At that moment the life blood drains out of the relationship. He wants porridge for breakfast, so she says, "Yes, dear, it's porridge for breakfast." So they *both* have porridge for breakfast. Or she wants to work in the yard every weekend, so rather than bicker, he says, "Yes, dear, we'll work in the yard." So they *both* work in the yard every weekend. Do these couples sound like Titty Mouse and Tatty Mouse? And yet, how many of us in our inability to cope with separateness, to reconcile differences, bring about this distorted situation? Like Titty and Tatty Mouse we haven't started out that way, but the irony is, in our attempt to smooth out differences between us, we come to this matrimonial monotony.

There are other paths that lead to a bloodless marriage. Imagine a situation in which one partner has been profoundly hurt or humiliated by some action of the other, such as an extra-marital love affair. This event takes on such enormous proportions that the partner who feels wronged finds no way to forgive and forget. No matter how remorseful the offender, he is met at every turn with a subtle reminder of his sin. Another situation is that of the man or woman who feels coerced into marriage by an unwanted pregnancy, parental pressure, or other social factors. Marcia and Chuck have been going together for three years, so if they broke up now, what would people say? A deep-seated hostility endures throughout the years. Eventually resentment and guilt are smothered by an apathetic silent adjustment, leading to an embittered, dispirited, and hollow existence.

For some couples the appeal of a Titty Tatty Mouse marriage lies in the security of an ordered life with no surprises. The man or woman who sees life as one huge mousetrap ready to spring is certainly not going to venture very far from customary paths. Even to smell the air for cheese becomes risky, and to risk is anathema to the fearful. Such people quickly discover a routine whereby life grinds away in habitual patterns. This evenness requires a lack of spontaneity; no movement, no passion is possible. On the other hand, no one can be hurt. Days may be predictable, life may be boring, but it is safe.

What happens if we let the boredom come through, experience it, and take the first tiny step toward what we are sure is the edge of the cliff? Our scene is set in suburbia. Titty Mouse and Tatty Mouse are at breakfast.

Ti. M. (Wearily) Sigh.

Ta. M. (Looks up briefly; sees nothing unusual, goes back to eating.)

Ti. M. Sigh.

Ta. M. (Without looking up) Anything wrong?

Ti. M. Not really. It's—Well—it's just this porridge.

Ta. M. What's wrong with the porridge?

Ti. M. Oh! Nothing's wrong with the porridge. It's delicious.

Ta. M. (With some impatience) Well?

Ti. M. Don't you ever get bored with porridge?

Ta. M. Bored? With porridge? What kind of a question is that? I never *think* about it. It's breakfast, that's all. We have to eat something.

Ti. M. I've been thinking about it and frankly, I'm bored with porridge.

Ta. M. Well now. You're acting crazy. All these years porridge has been fine, now you're *bored* with it.

Ti. M. (Absently) New Zealand.

Ta. M. What?

Ti. M. (Hesitantly) I heard that in New Zealand they have lamb chops and stewed tomatoes for breakfast.

Ta. M. (Astounded) Do I hear you right? Lamb chops and stewed tomatoes?! Do you know what that would cost? Do you know how much trouble that is to fix? Do you realize the dirty pans and dishes we'd have to wash? And what if someone came in and saw us eating lamb chops for breakfast? Besides, if you give in to this whim, who knows what you'll want next?

Anything here we've heard before? Quite a few familiar messages, aren't there: "Don't make a wave. I don't want to have to be concerned with you. Just let everything be all right." And, "You're crazy if you're different from me. New ideas are crazy." Plus, "What will people think?"

Although the issue is porridge, Tatty Mouse doesn't stick to that. Money, work, time, reputation all get dragged in. The only thing Tatty Mouse hasn't tried is threats. But we don't have to wait long:

"I can't live with such a mouse. Imagine! Porridge isn't good enough any more. My mother told me . . ."

Or possibly, "If you eat lamb chops and stewed tomatoes for breakfast, you won't have me across the table from you."

Branching out in breakfast foods is as risky as any other departure from your set, familiar ways. You open yourselves to charges of being extravagant, selfish, and crazy—all the things you're not supposed to be. You risk taking a stand. You risk being drawn into endless argument resulting in greater isolation. You risk upheaval. You risk intimacy.

Intimacy. The state we long for so desperately, and fear so totally. Great as our craving is to alleviate our essential aloneness, it is matched by our dread of being made vulnerable; to be intimate is to be vulnerable. When we expose completely how we feel or what we want, our partner might seize that opportunity to ridicule and accuse, to argue and threaten. Then we can be hurt; feel rejected and alone, unable to defend ourselves, unable to right a situation that we seem to have caused to go wrong. The paradox is that in attempting to draw nearer, we have ended up farther apart. For it takes two for intimacy to happen.

In this situation Titty Mouse has risked by taking a stand and talking about feelings and desires. Tatty Mouse either didn't know how, or didn't dare to be an intimate listener. Instead, Tatty used every tactic to avoid open listening. Listening openly can be as threatening as speaking openly. For when we hear, really hear, without arguments and our defenses to close us off, then we too become vulnerable, for we will be touched.

Same setting, Titty Mouse and Tatty Mouse at breakfast in suburbia.

Ta. M. You're up early this morning.

Ti. M. Yes, I'm fixing my breakfast. Doesn't it smell good?

Ta. M. You don't want porridge? Don't you love me anymore?

Ti. M. (Sighing) I'm bored with porridge. I feel like lamb chops and stewed tomatoes this morning. This has nothing to do with whether I love you or not. Can I fix you some?

Ta. M. I should say not! Whoever heard of such a breakfast?

A few minutes pass. The two quietly eat their respective breakfasts. An aroma rises from the frying pan.

Ta. M. (Sheepishly) Say, that does smell good. How about a taste, Love?

QUESTIONS FOR CHAPTER III

1. Are there ways you would like your partner to be like you? What are they?

2. How are you and your partner like Jack Sprat and his wife? In case you have forgotten:

   > Jack Sprat could eat no fat,
   > His wife could eat no lean;
   > And so betwixt them both, you see
   > They licked the platter clean.

3. Do you sometimes find yourself taking an extreme position in attitude or action that is opposed to your partner? What examples can you recall?

AWARENESS EXPERIENCES FOR CHAPTER III

1. Avoiding negative judgments, let each partner take a turn and name a quality or ability that your partner has *that you think you don't have.* Example: If you experience yourself as unselfish, and your partner as selfish, you might say: "You know what you want and how to get it." Another example: If you experience yourself as diplomatic, stretching the truth when it seems desirable, and your partner as overly frank and blunt, you might say: "You are always honest; you know how to call a spade a spade." Avoid generalities like: "You are open." Each take a turn and name a quality or ability that your partner has that you think you don't have. Remember, phrase it as a *positive* statement. Limit yourself to *one* statement each turn.

AWARENESS QUESTIONS:

How did you feel when your partner named your qualities or abilities?

Did you listen?

Did you want to explain, justify, or rationalize?

In your mind did you translate the positive statements about you into negative statements?

CHAPTER IV

THE FISHERMAN AND HIS WIFE

There was once a fisherman who lived with his wife in a pigsty, close by the seaside. The fisherman used to go out all day long a-fishing; and one day, as he sat on the shore with his rod, looking at the sparkling waves and watching his line, all of a sudden his float was dragged away deep into the water; and in drawing it up he pulled out a great fish. But the fish said, "Pray let me live! I am not a real fish! I am an enchanted prince; put me in the water again and let me go!" "Oh! ho!" said the man, "you need not make so many words about the matter; I will have nothing to do with a fish that can talk; so swim away, Sir, as soon as you please!" Then he put him back into the water, and the fish darted straight down to the bottom, and left a long streak of blood behind him on the wave.

When the fisherman went home to his wife in the pigsty, he told her how he had caught a great fish, and how it had told him it was an enchanted prince, and how, on hearing it speak, he had let it go again. "Did you not ask it for anything?" said the wife. "No," said the man; "what should I ask for?" "Ah!" said the wife, "we live very wretchedly here, in this nasty dirty pigsty; do go back and tell the fish we want a snug little cottage."

37

The fisherman did not much like the business; however, he went to the seashore, and when he came back there, the water looked all yellow and green. And he stood at the water's edge, and said,

> "O man of the sea!
> Hearken to me!
> My wife Ilsabill
> Will have her own will,
> And hath sent me to beg a boon of thee!"

Then the fish came swimming to him and said, "Well, what is her will? What does your wife want?" "Ah!" said the fisherman, "she says that when I had caught you, I ought to have asked you for something before I let you go; she does not like living any longer in the pigsty, and wants a snug little cottage." "Go home, then," said the fish; "she is in the cottage already!" So the man went home and saw his wife standing at the door of a nice trim little cottage.

Well, it is not long before the fisherman's wife is discontented with the cottage. She asks for, and receives, a large stone castle. Then, of course, she demands to be king, then emperor, then pope. With each demand, the sea becomes darker and more threatening; the fisherman more afraid. Finally, the wife demands to be lord of the sun and the moon.

> "Alas, wife!" said he, "cannot you be easy with being pope?" "No," said she, "I am very uneasy as long as the sun and moon rise without my leave. Go to the fish at once!"

Then the man went shivering with fear; and as he was going down to the shore a dreadful storm arose, so that the trees and the very rocks shook. And all the heavens became black with stormy clouds, and the lightning played, and the thunders rolled; and you might have seen in the sea great black waves, swelling up like mountains with crowns of white foam upon their heads. And the fisherman crept towards the sea and cried out, as well as he could,

> "O man of the sea!
> Hearken to me!
> My wife Ilsabill
> Will have her own will,
> And hath sent me to beg a boon of thee!"

"What does she want now?" said the fish, "Ah!" said he, "she wants to be lord of the sun and moon." "Go home," said the fish, "to your pigsty again."

And there they live to this very day.

We find here an extremely demanding wife paired with a man who will do anything to indulge her—a perfect combination, at first glance, and yet a closer look uncovers two frustrated people, neither getting what he wants. Indeed, the wife has no idea what she really desires. She demands instant gratification of every whim, but each acquisition affords only temporary satisfaction. She is unable to enjoy anything that she has and is totally preoccupied with what she still imagines she needs. Possessed by her greediness, she is doomed to an empty, futile life of discontentment. This type of person lives her life unaware of those around her, their needs, feelings, and desires. In her self-centeredness, she is like a child who has learned only the words, "I want."

The fisherman's wife imagines that material possessions and power will fill up her emptiness. She demands these. Other wives of this type imagine that if only they could have more freedom, or more attention, or more affection, or more control over how their husbands behave they would be content. Unfortunately, such people are insatiable. With each demand that is granted, a new demand follows on its heels with the wife always dangling the implicit promise like a carrot on a stick, that when this latest wish is met, she will be *happy*. When she is happy, her husband can expect her to be concerned with his wishes, which she has, up to this point, either not noticed or consciously ignored.

The fisherman's wife is blatant in her demands. He does not have to play guessing games, wondering exactly what is the gift, the circumstance, the action that will bring an end to his wife's discontentment. Other husbands, not given such explicit directions, are constantly frustrated in their efforts to please. They try one method after another while their wives sit back waiting for them to do the wrong thing. By this form of manipulation, wives can stay in complete control of their husbands, doling out favors just often enough to keep bait in their traps.

The wife in this story will not permit her commands to go unfulfilled. The fisherman does not want to go to the fish asking for more and more favors, but what alternative does he have? He knows his wife. He knows he will have no peace, that she will not give him a moment's rest until he does her bidding. He can argue with her, reason with her, try substitutes, but she has a fixed idea, a notion that grows to such proportions that all perspective is lost. Such wives are experts at emotional blackmail. They know how to extort what they want from their husbands. Some, like the fisherman's wife, make vociferous demands; some sit back and pout; some withhold sex; some angrily or quietly nag. The results are the same. The husbands allow themselves to be put in the position of being overly responsible for their wives' happiness. Needless to say, this situation frequently occurs in reverse with a demanding husband who is not satisfied no matter how much his wife caters to him.

40

What kind of man takes upon himself this thankless task, a lifelong challenge of satisfying a greedy, ambitious, insatiable woman? This is a man who needs, more than anything else, the gratification which comes from the pat on the head which says, "You've done well, you have put my wishes first, you have brought me pleasure. Now I will love you." Unfortunately for our fisherman, this reward never comes. His deep craving for approval is accompanied by a constant dread of disapproval, so that he will act against his own better judgment, against his own conscience, in order to avoid his wife's displeasure. The fisherman faces the angry, boiling sea and makes outrageous requests of the fish rather than say, "No!" to his wife. We see that he lacks will and self-assertion. All of his actions are directed toward gaining the support he expects will someday be forthcoming from his wife. He has no power of his own. He cannot take a stand.

The fisherman and his wife have an implicit contractual agreement that can be summed up like this: her desires take precedence over his desires; he must indulge her demands; he remains a spineless man, working to gain the love and appreciation of his wife; he evades taking responsibility for his actions. The fisherman and his wife are like the characters that play parts in the other folktales; all are living up to unspoken agreements.

Such agreements are typical of all relationships. In fact, some therapists and marriage counselors have experimented with bringing these arrangements out into the open through *explicit* contracts in order to facilitate the give and take necessary in intimate relationships. For instance, a wife demands that her husband talk to her for a specified amount of time when he comes home from work. The husband agrees, providing his wife is available for sex twice a week. What

41

kind of conversation, what kind of sex results from a contractual agreement? The chances seem slight that such contracts could lead to spirited, mutually satisfying interaction, or could open the door to new and different ways of behaving. It seems more likely that patterns of withholding will emerge, for although you can contract actions, it is a certainty that you cannot contract feelings.

Overheard at the beach:

Older Woman: "What did you make John for dinner last night?"

Younger woman describes in great detail a superb meal.

Older Woman: "Did he like it?"

Younger Woman: "I have to pry it out of him. 'Do you like it? Do you like it? Do you like it?' 'Yup.' And this morning the first thing he says is, 'What are we having for dinner tonight?' I told him, 'Fuck you. I'm not cooking for you no more. You don't appreciate it."

The operative contract for her is: "I'll cook meals for you. You must express appreciation for my efforts." Unfortunately for this couple, it is a unilateral contract of which the husband has not been informed.

Part of the process of living and growing together is to make explicit what we want from ourselves and our partner. Clear understanding must reflect the growing awareness of ourselves, each other, and changing situations. We are complicated individuals with contradictory needs and desires. We give double messages: "Let me lean on you. Let me be independent." "I want to love only you. I want to be free to love others."

Our messages are inconsistent, because our feelings are inconsistent. Some of our needs are below any level of awareness. Out of a buried past come hidden longings and wishes which could never be made explicit. They are out of reach of our consciousness, yet they can powerfully influence our actions, our words, and our disappointments. A person might be aware of a desire to be loved and appreciated, and at the same time be oblivious to a suppressed urge to be punished. Perhaps the fisherman suffers this ambivalence.

Ambivalence in ourselves is confusing enough. To live with it in a partner can be sheer torture. Consider the case of Jack, a young man who insists that he wants to marry Polly. He goes to Europe to spend four months traveling on business. He writes repeatedly pleading with her to write to him, but he doesn't give her an address. He contends that he wants her with him, but never makes this possible. She is left confused by his ardent letters that have no return address. Is he only "giving her a line?" No, he is of two minds and expresses both to her. One he takes responsibility for and expresses openly; the other makes itself known through his oversights.

Frequently we are not conscious of the contracts we are living by until we run into a disappointment. "I married you for companionship and now you're never home." "I supported your folks during their hard times, now you won't even have my mother visit us." "I never complained when you worked overtime. How come you get mad when I want to work on one Saturday morning?" "I went fishing with you last year. This year I thought you'd go to the city with me." "I always offer to rub your back and you never offer to rub mine." "I was miserable as a kid. I thought when I married you everything would be nice." (Which translated means that *you* are supposed to make up for my unhappy childhood.) Without ever telling the other person *what* we expect, we imagine that we'll be repaid for what we do. We keep our end of the bargain but our partner doesn't. He doesn't even know there's a bargain!

The fisherman's contract with his wife includes his not taking a stand. Before he can do that, the fisherman must have a sure feeling of himself, his "I," his identity. "*I* want." "*I* believe." "*I* feel." "*I* am an important person." Then he will gradually begin to discover his own substantial foundation so that he can eventually literally stand on his feet, assume his position and say, "Here I stand."

Notice the words the fisherman uses in his requests of the fish: "My wife Ilsabill will have her own will and hath sent me to beg a boon of thee." He does his *wife's* bidding. He takes no responsibility for his actions. He can't be blamed. We frequently see this type of behavior in men who commit robbery or other crimes. When questioned, they often say that their wife wanted a better house, or a fur coat, or a trip to Europe. The phrase, "Behind every great man is a woman," is related to this same phenomenon. Some men are propelled to success on their wives' ambition; others to ignominy.

The fisherman and his wife are in a tragic situation. They are sailing in rocky waters, and it would seem hopeless that they could ever have a harmonious, satisfying relationship. Yet it is tempting to stop them for a moment in their lives and help them experience what they are doing to themselves and each other. They then might awake from their nightmarish existence and discover a world in which they have some alternative and mutually satisfying ways of being with each other.

After the magic fish grants their first wish, the couple find themselves in a comfortable cottage with a garden and fruit trees. The wife quickly becomes bored and wants more. At this point, let us replay the scene. The fisherman takes a stand. No, he will not make any further requests of the fish. He will no longer abide by the implicit contract. Let his wife have a tantrum, nag, ignore him, he will not give in.

Now he is doing them both a favor. At this moment he is discovering his own identity. By refusing to be manipulated by his wife's childish ploys, he can frustrate her to the point where she might switch from the track of habitual responses to the difficult but exciting track of growth and change. Of course, her choice, at this moment of frustration, may be to find herself another fisherman who is more easily controlled. This is a risk the fisherman takes.

Now let us continue with our pretending. The wife is stymied. How can she manipulate her husband now? How can she get what she wants? Her husband is a different man. And when she looks at him she sees a different man. She sees someone who perceives her, who cares about her. But if he cares about her, why won't he ask the fish for a castle? Because he also cares about himself, including his values, his morals, his conscience.

Now is her opportunity to experience her frustration rather than frantically turning to some action or some plan to avoid it. To suffer her frustration in its totality means to confront a frightening and overwhelming void. She finds herself face to face with the basic questions of existence: Who am I? Where am I? What is the meaning of life? For centuries philosophers, poets, and theologians have wrestled with these questions. Is there a chance that our poor fisherman's wife can deal with them? Simply facing the void forces her to recognize that it is not a reservoir to be filled with streams of more and more possessions and power, but a human condition, shared to some extent by all. Her world becomes like a landscape that has been buried under fog. Now the mist gradually lifts and she has the chance to discover herself, her husband, her house, and garden. The emptiness she has known, without her trying to fill it or fight it, will gradually diminish as she becomes truly engaged with life.

QUESTIONS FOR CHAPTER IV

1. Do you have anything in common with Ilsabill? With the fisherman?

2. Did you ever want something very much, get it, and find you were disappointed? When was this?

3. When did you last say "no" to a request of your partner? Was this difficult? Did you think you had to apologize?

AWARENESS EXPERIENCES FOR CHAPTER IV

Each person make a list of three things that you would ask of the magic fish. Don't tell or show your list. When each has completed the list of three, take turns and guess what three things are on the other's list. (It's all right if you guessed incorrectly. Go on to the next part.) Then, after you have guessed, exchange lists and talk about the wishes. Avoid asking "why" questions. (Example: Why do you want an avocado orchard? Avocado trees get diseases, you know.)

AWARENESS QUESTIONS:

When you guessed each other's lists, did you guess any correctly?

Were you interested to hear your partner's wishes?

Do you experience your partner's wishes as demands that you must *do* something about?

Did you feel guilty, resentful, happy, when you heard the other's wishes?

Can you talk about your feelings?

Avoid arguments. Just listen, and share.

TO FALL IN LOVE

CHAPTER V

THE HALF-CUP OF TEA

The Half-Cup of Tea

There was once a man who always complained that whenever he asked for a half-cup of tea he always got a full one. No woman, he said, could pour out a half-cup of tea; and if he met one who could he'd marry her because she'd be a wonder. Well, one day he went to a garden party, and a young lady whom he hadn't met before was helping his hostess.

She asked him if he'd like another cup of tea, and he said, "Just half, please."

She poured him out exactly half. He looked at her with great respect, and he thought she was a very pretty girl. He found out her name, and he saw a lot of her after that, and liked her more and more, and in the end he asked her to marry him. They were married, and on the honeymoon she said, "What made you first think of me?"

"Well, do you remember the first day we met?" said her husband, "when I asked you for half a cup of tea?"

"Oh, yes," she said, "I remember. There wasn't a drop more in the pot, and I was so ashamed."

49

What has this man done? He has chosen his life's partner on very flimsy evidence indeed—a woman who will pour a half cup of tea when he requests it. The idea that a woman who will do this must surely be unusually fine and desirable has grown in his mind until reason, logic and actual experience may have nothing to do with his decision. "Any woman who will pour a half cup of tea will be the woman for me." "Any man who is so kind to dogs will make a wonderful husband." "A woman who is well groomed and keeps her house so clean will make any man a good wife." And so we "fall in love."

The romantic notion of "falling in love" interferes with the development of a relationship of growing and genuine love. Falling in love is more often a disguise for sexual desire, a craving for intimacy. Through the screen of our need and desire we see only dimly who this other person is; we marry a fantasy, a creation constructed to fit our requirements, a concept in place of a person. When people marry concepts and hold on to these concepts, the deep understanding that can grow through sharing a life together never has a chance even to begin. Their expectations lead to disappointment, to blaming, to maneuvers that lead away from, rather than towards, true contact between two persons.

To begin with, we are cursed with two separate categories of expectations: one has to do with *marriage;* the other pertains to the particular *individual* whom we choose as a partner. The media constantly sell us the fairytale promise of living happily ever after; and even though we know differently, our tendency is to identify with the comforting message that "every day will be a holiday because I'm married to you." We imagine that *our* marriage will be different, better than those unhappy relationships we have seen our parents and friends struggling with, because we are truly in love. There are as many dreams as there are individuals who venture into an intimate relationship, but surely the most widespread is also the one least possible to realize: that of a miracle, a Garden of Eden existence of supreme happiness without frustrations. The disagreements and conflicts that we have experienced before marriage, we trust, will be dealt with lovingly and reasonably, and love and reason, like magic wands, will cause all unpleasantness to vanish. Of course we all know better, and in sober discussion agree that marriage won't always be easy; it requires work, commitment, maturity and wisdom. Yet this intelligent attitude neither eases our profound disappointment nor lessens our disillusionment when we discover that marital bliss is a familiar phrase but an unfamiliar state.

The second category of expectations deals directly with ourselves and our partner, and we need to consider briefly how men and women see each other and themselves. Women have for centuries been portrayed as saints or sinners, as madonnas or prostitutes. These traditional stereotypes have left their mark on men as well as on women. Men have been the fighters, the providers, and the protectors. Such established notions of masculinity and femininity still can interfere with a full discovery of ourselves and our mates. What we actually know about the one we choose to marry is extremely limited, both because of lack of exposure in a realistic living situation and through our efficient process of selecting what we choose to see and hear. The tea drinker "looked at her with great respect" and saw what he wanted to see, a very pretty girl. We ignore those aspects which don't mesh with our fantasy and supercharge the other person with traits that will in some way make up for our own deficiencies.

If I doubt my own soundness, I am likely to see in my partner a wholesomeness and degree of sanity that may or may not be present. At any rate, I expect that *his* soundness will make *me* more normal. In effect, I marry in order that my partner will make me sane. Alternatively, I may find someone who makes me feel lovable, or sexually competent, or strong, or successful, or important. In any of these situations, I am marrying a person in order that he can do something specific *for me*. I am making my partner *responsible* for my sanity or my ability to love, to be successful, competent, or any of a variety of capacities and capabilities which I lack, or imagine I lack.

Frequently we choose for our partner someone whose presence in our life reproduces a familiar, although not necessarily satisfying, pattern of existence. We put ourselves into a situation similar to that which we have known, perhaps as a child. A man married to a woman who keeps him guessing whether or not she loves him, whether or not she will stay with him, may discover that this is a replay of his boyhood existence with his mother. A woman who marries a wife-beater may have had a father who beat her. These are only two examples of life scripts, of programs into which people become fixed. There seems to be an irresistible urge for people *unconsciously* to repeat such situations, hoping through these efforts to work successfully through them. This may seem an absurd and self-torturing approach to living, yet it is important to realize that people who are captive to a single scheme of life have lost sight of, or have never seen, other possibilities. When the primary function of a marriage is to finish up an unfinished life situation, the marriage usually fails on both counts.

Disappointment is bound to follow the illusions we have

of marriage and the fantasized expectations we have for ourselves and our partners. What will the husband do when he finds out the "truth" about his wife who poured him the half cup of tea? One possibility is that he'll feel deceived, for he has constructed a fantasy for himself, a bubble which his wife has just popped. None of us likes to have our bubbles popped. When this happens he is apt to feel rather stupid—but only momentarily. He will quickly cover up this unflattering opinion of himself, probably with an attack on his partner who did this terrible thing to him. She will no doubt wonder at the vehemence of his outburst, and may sadly realize that the honeymoon is already over.

If, on the other hand, the two of them used the period between the garden party and the honeymoon to get to know one another in a frank, straightforward, undesigning manner rather than being blinded by expectations and fantasies, the husband might enjoy the humor of the situation, recognize the absurdity of his obsession, and consider himself lucky.

How long does it take for reality to push through to our awareness, for the blaming to begin? When our deficiencies remain, when our minuses are not cancelled out by the pluses we imagined to exist in our partner, we seldom have the self-knowledge or integrity to be honest. It would be a rare person who would say to his mate: "Your strength is supposed to be an antidote for my weakness. Where is it?"

Again and again couples are about to make contact, but slide past each other, narrowly missing. Each time we slip into measuring our partner against some expectation of how he should be, or what he should do for us, we fail to get past the screen and the distortions we ourselves create. "Be what I imagine you are. Live up to my fantasy," is a frequent demand of partners, but is rarely spoken out loud. A wife,

53

struggling against the net of her husband's expectations, described her situation vividly: "I always had to be 'a big girl' for my mother. My husband married me thinking I was a big girl, but he doesn't know there's a little child inside."

A sound marriage begins by connecting to the reality of this other person, by genuinely appreciating who our partner is. This comes with contact over a period of time. Real contact involves letting go of our expectations and seeing and hearing another as he *is*, not as we wish him to be, not how we dreamed or imagined him to be. Acceptance and understanding are what we all want and what we find so difficult to have, totally, for another.

A genuine appreciation depends to a large degree on our undisguised experience of who *we* are in relation to this other person. This recognition and acknowledgment of ourselves and the other is an on-going process, during which we discover differences between ourselves and our partners. We will experience times when our individual boundaries almost seem to disappear, and times when they are very much there, not as a wall that comes between us, but rather as points of contact. This idea may become clearer if you remember what happens when you hold someone's hand for a period of time without moving. After a while you no longer feel the other hand. There is still contact, since your hands are still together, but you no longer *experience* the contact. The boundaries are lost. You have to move your hand to make sure you are still touching. In a relationship, true contact begins with an appreciation of differences, a recognition of boundaries. You are you, and I am I. And that is how we know we are touching one another.

When couples cease to refer to themselves separately and speak always of "we" ("we don't like fish," "we like to

54

go to bed early," "we always vote Republican"), it is a sign that the essential boundary is being obliterated. Individuality is in danger of being lost. No two people always have the same attitudes, see situations the same way, like the same people, food, television programs, and books. Individuals agree and disagree. They experience a given situation differently. Each has his own insight, judgment, intuition; his own eyes, ears, and bloodstream; his own taste, his own *self*.

When Henry Higgins asks in *My Fair Lady,* "Why can't a woman be like me?" he expresses what all of us feel at one time or another when our partner's differences make appreciation difficult. How frustrating to find someone with another "right way" to do something! How irritating to be met with logic when we know logic is irrelevant at this moment, or to face emotion when we know logic is what makes sense!

Ideally, each individual in a marriage has his own existence, closely involved with, but separate from, that of his partner. When is a problem my problem? When is it my partner's problem? Or is it always a shared problem? A person comes into marriage with his life, his skein of yarn, tangled in parts, knotted in parts, weak in places, strong in places. His partner comes with her skein of yarn, also tangled and knotted. The two skeins join together, become intertwined, sometimes blending, sometimes complementing, sometimes with colors clashing, yarns tangling. Joint problems show as the two colors knotting together; when knots of one skein connect with knots of the other skein, which is so often the case, then to separate the intertwined problems to deal with them separately becomes an enormous challenge. Can I be unaffected by your problems? How do I feed into your problems?

Each partner, to a degree, furnishes some material for the other's problems. Just as the ogre's wife feeds into her

55

husband's tyranny by her attitude and actions, we have subtle but acute ways of affecting and undermining our partners. We become involved in their problems. The reformed alcoholic's wife frequently claims his old habit.

Trying to solve other people's problems is generally useless. We can say, "If I were you, I would . . ." Invariably the other says, "Yes, BUT . . ." And it once again becomes clear I am not you; what I imagine I would do in a similar situation you would not consider doing. A well-meaning mate who takes responsibility for finding a solution for his partner's problems, whatever they may be—alcoholism, obesity, impatience, irresponsibility—will inevitably meet with frustration and usually outright sabotage. A wife who puts her ostensibly complying husband on a diet, and discovers candy wrappers in the car is up against underhand interference.

Marriage is like two people paddling a canoe. What each does affects what the other does. There's a great deal more to it than pouring a cup of tea.

QUESTIONS FOR CHAPTER V

1. Do you remember a fairy tale from childhood? Does it have significance in your life now?

2. What words of wisdom did you hear from your parents that you would pass on to your children about the man or woman who would make a good mate? What would you *not* pass on?

3. What advice that you got do you think is foolish now?

AWARENESS EXPERIENCES FOR CHAPTER V

1. In the story, the young bride asks, "What made you first think of me?" Discuss together what you first noticed about each other. Did you see what you wanted to see?

2. Sit facing each other; close your eyes and relax for a moment. Now open your eyes and see each other as five years old. Do not talk during this part. After one or two minutes, close your eyes. Become aware of how you feel. After a few moments, open your eyes and talk about this.

3. Again sit relaxed with your eyes closed for a few moments. Now open your eyes and see each other as 75 years old. No talking now. After one or two minutes, close your eyes again. How do you feel? Now open your eyes and talk about this.

Note: Do not "make faces" to *try* to look a particular age. Let each simply look and use his imagination.

AWARENESS QUESTIONS:

Did you speak openly or did you withhold in order to protect your partner's feelings?

Are you listening while your partner talks or are you thinking about what you want to say? Or is your mind busy with something else?

CHAPTER VI

STUPID MEN AND SHREWISH WIVES

Stupid Men and Shrewish Wives

There were once two wives who were always quarreling, the way some wives do now and then, and, as they had nothing better to quarrel about, they started bickering about their husbands: about which one was the stupidest of the two. The longer they quarreled, the angrier they grew, and at last they were on the verge of coming to blows. For one thing is certain: "A quarrel is more easily stirred than stilled, and it's a bad thing when common sense is lacking."

The first wife said that there was not a thing she could not make her husband believe if she but said it was true, for he was gullible as the trolls! And the second wife said that no matter how wrong it might be, she could make her husband do anything if she said it should be done, for he was the kind who could not see through a ladder.

"Well, let's see which one of us can fool them the best. Then we'll find out which husband is the stupidest," they said, and this they agreed to do.

Now, when her husband came home from the woods, the

first wife cried, "Heaven help me! Why, this is awful! You must be sick, if you're not already dying!"

"There's nothing wrong with me that food and drink won't cure!" said the man.

"God save me if it isn't true!" sobbed the wife. "It's getting worse and worse all right; you look as pale as a corpse. You'd better lie down! Oh, you won't last long at all!"

Thus she carried on until she got the man to believe that he was at death's door. She got him to lie down, fold his hands, and close his eyes. Then she stretched him out, put him in a shroud, and laid him in a coffin. But, so he would not suffocate while he was in there, she made some holes in the boards so he could breathe and peek out.

The other wife, she took a pair of carders, sat down, and started carding. But she had no wool on them. Her husband came in and looked at what she was doing.

"It helps little to spin without a wheel, but to card without wool, a wife is a fool," said the man.

"Without wool?" said the wife. "Why, of course I have wool, but you can't see it because it's the finest kind!"

When she had finished carding, she got out the spinning wheel and started to spin.

"Nay! This is going right to the dogs!" said the man. "Why, you're sitting there whirling and spoiling your wheel without anything on it!"

"Without anything on it?" said the wife. "The thread is so fine that it takes better eyes than yours to see it."

When she had finished spinning, she set up the loom and threaded it and wove the cloth. Then she took it off the loom, and cut it out, and sewed clothes out of it for her husband. And when they were finished she hung them up in the *stabbur* loft. The man could see neither cloth nor clothes, but now he had come to believe that they were so fine that he could not see them, and so he said, "Well, well, as long as they're so fine, it's lucky I am to have them."

But one day his wife said to him, "Today you must go to a burial feast. The man at the North farm is getting buried today, so you have to have on your new clothes." Well, well, go to the burial feast he should, and the wife helped him on with the clothes, for they were so fine that he would tear them to pieces if he did it himself.

When he came up to the farm to the burial feast, they had already been drinking hard and fast, and their grief was not any greater when they caught sight of him with his new church-going clothes on, I dare say.

But as they were on the way to the graveyard, and the dead man peeked out through the breathing holes, he almost split his sides laughing. "Well, now I have to laugh!" he said. "If it isn't old Ola South Farm at my burial feast as naked as the day he was born!"

When people in the funeral procession heard that, it did not take them long to get the lid off the coffin. And the one with the new church-going clothes on asked how it could be that he lay in the coffin, talking and laughing, when they were holding a burial feast for him. Why, it would be more fitting if he cried.

"Tears never dug anyone up out of the grave," said the other. But the longer they talked together, the more clear it became that the wives had arranged the whole thing between them. So the husbands went home and did the wisest thing they had ever done. And if anybody wants to know what that was, then he'd better ask the birch rod!

Wives fooling husbands is a classic subject often used in folktales. We have already met the ogre's wife in Chapter II, the underdog wife who uses whatever resources are available to avoid her husband's anger or withdrawal. Wives have traditionally used their power in devious ways, for our culture has demanded that men must appear to have the power in a relationship. Constructing stories, feigning emotions, and resorting to underhanded manipulations are time-honored ways that wives have used in real life as well as in folktales to achieve their goals and satisfy their needs for power.

When our story begins the women are arguing about which one has the more stupid husband. Wives frequently enjoy this kind of "can you top this" activity, a combination of boasting and complaining which serves as a safety valve to prevent resentments toward husbands from becoming too overwhelming. In addition to dispelling boredom, attempting to outdo another reassures that other wives have similar dissatisfactions and other husbands similar shortcomings. A successful session of "look what I have to put up with" can leave a woman wonderfully purged and comforted.

It is a commentary on these two wives that they choose to compete with each other through discrediting their husbands. Do they imagine that they raise themselves up by putting their husbands down? Or is this retaliation? The tasks they have chosen are clearly examples of colossal public humiliation for their husbands: the first husband is literally "put down." These women are not content to deride their men behind their backs or in private; they do it in front of the entire community.

The central point of the story, however, concerns the responses of the men: their inability to be aware of their own perceptions and experiences, and to trust the validity of those perceptions and experiences, even when others may disagree. The wives are very convincing and their husbands allow themselves to be persuaded that their wives know better then they do what is happening to them. The first husband takes his wife's word for how *he* feels. The second allows his wife to tell him what *he* sees. When they accept information that contradicts their own experiences, the men are in danger.

Feeling and seeing, indeed the excitement of any sense or emotion, is an individual's way of responding to what is happening in the world around him. When a person rejects or denies his subjective experience he relinquishes to some degree his ability to respond. Literally, he gives up response / ability and depends on someone else to tell him how he is or how the world is; to respond *for* him.

The first husband allows his wife to convince him that he is ready to be put in a coffin. While certainly an extreme, it is in no way unusual for A to convince B that he or she is stupid, or doesn't know how to handle children, or has no sense of values, or taste in clothes, or ability to handle money, or sensitivity in sexual matters. Usually there is an additional notion that improvement is out of the question in these areas. "You'll never change." But luckily A can take over. These are common examples of one spouse's insisting that he knows how the other is, or should be; feels, or should feel. Insults or indignation aimed at another's subjective experience, at another's ability to respond, tend to diminish a person and erode his sense of self. As a person's sense of self is weakened he comes to rely more and more on the other to respond for him, to take responsibility for him. He surrenders himself piecemeal, gradually giving over custody of himself to his partner.

This process does not begin in marriage; it's a pattern often begun by parents. They disenfranchise their children by denying them their rights as separate individuals with their subjective reality. Childhood is the time when we learn to trust the validity of our own experiences, to trust our perceptions and intuitions; it is also the time when we can be deprived of this ability to trust ourselves through a lack of affirmation from those around us. Too often our experiences in school corroborate the attitude that someone else knows better than we what we want, what we need, and how we are: that someone outside of ourselves will take responsibility for us.

When you give up responding, and substitute the judgment of another for your subjective experience, you relinquish some measure of control over yourself and your life. This is one of the easy paths to the "blaming" trap. Once you give up responsibility—hand it over—that person becomes the target for your failures. Your words and actions are no longer the expressions of your feelings and thoughts, but rather attempts to meet demands and desires of another. Instead of *expressing* yourself, you're *impressing* others. What a trap this is for both partners!

The shrewish wives take advantage of more than their husbands' stupidity. They abuse the trust their husbands have in them. The issue of trust is not simple. What does it mean to trust another? Trust is part of all our personal folklore: "I thought I could trust you." "Now I'll never be able to trust you again." "Do you trust me? Well, there's nothing to worry about, is there?'' "My mother told me I shouldn't trust you."

Familiar lines all, but what do they mean? Is the meaning the same for the speaker and the receiver? "I thought I could trust you" usually means, "I was relying on you to live up to my expectations." To the receiver it suggests something different, accusation and blame: "You have been a bad person and I don't know whether I can ever love you again." What is there to say to this threat of abandonment and loneliness? It leads inevitably to guilt and defensiveness. "I'm sorry. I'll never do that again," or, "I don't care. I don't need you anyway;" neither totally true.

"Trust" is a hazy idea in marriage, difficult to talk about in specific terms. We *know* when we trust our partner by our feelings when we're with him or thinking about him. These feelings are based on certain assumptions about people in general, and our mate, in particular.

When our trust is abused, has the other person failed us? Or have our faulty assumptions led us astray?

A wife relates that her husband was extremely upset with her when he discovered a blatant lie that she told. Her retort, much to his astonishment, was, "I never said I was honest." The safety of any assumptions about your partner depends on how well you know him. The calculated dishonesty of the shrewish wives will most likely keep their husbands on guard in the future. By their experience, unless the husbands are more stupid than we already know, they will have learned something about their wives that will make their future assumptions about them more realistic. They won't be so gullible.

There is the key. The more we know about someone, the

more our trust in him is based on reality instead of our fantasy.

Apart from the calculated dishonesty of the story, there is the dishonesty that results from unawareness of one's own intentions. "I will never do that again," can be said with sincerity at one moment; you have made a promise; you have "every intention" of keeping it. Then what happens? You find yourself breaking your word. It's as if there are two you's working against each other. In effect, integrity rests upon self awareness.

The word "promise" brings up another point. Sometimes we hear a promise when none is given. Consider this example: Shortly after marriage, a woman, disturbed by dreams of her father who had recently died, wanted to see a therapist. Her husband ridiculed the idea with such vehemence that she was persuaded not to seek help. During the ensuing years she experienced several occasions when she would have liked to consult a professional, but, knowing how her husband felt about therapists, she "rose above" her problems and carried on as he expected her to. She was getting the unspoken message from her husband, "I can solve my problems and I expect you to do the same. I would never go for professional help." Meanwhile her husband began to suffer severe depression and on the advice of a friend he consulted a therapist. When he told his wife that he had been seeing a counselor she became furious. Her violent reaction astounded and confused him. He couldn't appreciate that she experienced his action as a colossal deception.

Here is another example of hearing a promise when none is given: Early in their life together a wife hears her husband remark about a colleague: "That bastard is cheating on his wife and she is such a sweet person, too." She hears: "As long as you are a sweet wife I won't show interest in any other woman. I would be a bastard to do a thing like that." The husband has promised nothing; his wife has twisted his statement into the promise she wants to hear. When this "promise" is broken, she feels doubly cheated. She has been the sweetest wife she knows how to be for five, ten, or twenty-five years, only to discover that she apparently hasn't come up to her husband's expectations. Not only does she not get the promised reward, a faithful husband, but she is left feeling that she is somehow the guilty one as well as the victim of being married to a bastard.

Both of these wives have felt the rug pulled out from under them. But we know from every one of the folktales, that *both* partners play a part in what goes on between them. The husbands in these examples may have done the pulling, but the wives have positioned themselves smack in the middle of the rugs.

We want to trust our partners to live up to marriage contracts, even when these are not made explicit, to trust them to keep promises we have heard them make, although no promise has been given. We want to trust them to be honest, even when honesty requires a degree of personal integration which they may have not yet achieved.

Perhaps ultimately we can trust only that each one will be uniquely himself, a person with all the qualities and capacities that people have to be tender, and callous; weak, and strong; to be serene, and stormy; cooperative, and resistant; loving, and indifferent; or any of a thousand other qualities. Ideally, we can trust one another only to be responding, responsible people, people who have left their rigid concepts of themselves and each other behind and accept flexibility and change.

Our folktale of "Stupid Men and Shrewish Wives" ends with the men taking up the birch rod, not an unusual ending for folktales. Men have in almost every case had a physical advantage over women; they have used this threat implicitly or explicitly. Women, in contrast, have developed powers of intrigue and sabotage, as we have seen in this and other tales. To argue which came first is an unproductive exercise in mental gymnastics which does nothing to resolve differences between partners.

As in every marriage where couples are stuck in defending and blaming we hear: "If you hadn't done that I wouldn't have done this." "Yes, but you did this first, that's why I did that." Or, "If you weren't this way I wouldn't be that way." So women can say: "If men didn't have their superior physical strength to fall back on, we wouldn't have to be devious." And men can reply: "If you women were straight out with your feelings we wouldn't be so frustrated that we have to resort to using force." Again we hear: "I'm not to blame, it's your fault." Until we move beyond defending and blaming, beyond wanting simple, easy answers, we remain stuck, spinning our wheels in rigid, joyless relationships.

Simple, easy answers are what we learned in first grade. It's hard to leave behind the definite, the clear, and the positive—that which we found proven in textbooks. In an intimate relationship the subject matter is *you:* ambiguous, complex, variable, changeable. All you have to go on is your own experience. Armed with that, you can, in ways that are sometimes awkward and bumbling, because you are human, move responsively and responsibly toward and away from one another.

QUESTIONS FOR CHAPTER VI

1. Have you ever substituted another's judgment about you for your own experience of yourself?

2. Did you come to agree with this judgment?

3. Whom in your life do you trust the most?

4. What are some of the things you trust this person to do or not to do?

AWARENESS EXPERIENCES FOR CHAPTER VI

Keep this experience light and even humorous. Play with it; make it fun.

Sit facing each other. Choose which person will begin. Take turns making one statement, starting your sentence with, "Look what I have to put up with . . ."

Example: Look what I have to put up with, a partner who snores!

Example: Look what I have to put up with, a partner who leaves his socks on the floor!

Example: Look what I have to put up with, a partner who burns potatoes!

Continue taking turns until you have no more "Look what I have to put up withs."

AWARENESS QUESTIONS:

Were any of your partner's statements hurtful to you? Can you share this, without defending yourself and without blaming your partner?

If your partner tells that one or more of your statements hurt, can you simply *listen* and hear what is being said, without defending yourself and without blaming your partner?

This experience was meant to be light. Could you do it in that spirit?

CHAPTER VII

THE MASTER

The Master

A man was married to a shrew who ordered him around the livelong day. Once, when she had several women friends calling on her, she wanted to show off before them what absolute control she had over her husband.

"*Schlemihl*," she ordered, "get under the table!" Without a word the man crawled under the table.

"Now, *Schlemihl*, come out!" she again commanded.

"I won't, I won't!" he defied her angrily. "I'll show you that I'm still master in this house!"

An unlikely place from which to assert one's power! If he were standing on his feet shouting his defiance from the top of the table, Schlemihl might command our attention rather than our laughter. But he is under the table and in a double bind. If he stays there, he continues to be a Schlemihl. If he comes out, he is following his wife's command and he's still a Schlemihl. Nonetheless, from his unfortunate position under

71

the table he informs his wife that she can no longer take his compliance for granted: he defies her with his words and his actions.

Partners always have mutually accepted rules that govern how they are with each other: who makes requests, who makes decisions, who gets angry, who makes peace. These rules are seldom made explicit; they are rarely discussed in the open. Mr. and Mrs. Schlemihl never specifically agreed that she was the boss and that he had to follow her orders, yet they both understand the rules and comply with them. When the rules of the game are observed by both players, nothing goes amiss. Up to now, this would seem to have been the case for the couple in this story.

Suddenly Schlemihl is shouting, "I won't!" from under the table. Without this response, they wouldn't have any change in their marriage, and *we* wouldn't have a story. Every story, and every renegotiation of rules, proceeds from a change in equilibrium. We have a story because Schlemihl unexpectedly decides he won't go along with the game. Mrs. Schlemihl has herself provoked the crisis by stretching the rules: she orders her husband around in front of her friends. She has increased the cast of characters from the customary two. Schlemihl now loses face in front of his wife's friends.

He defies her. He lets his wife know that he does not accept the change in rules. And if *he* does not go along, the change is not possible. For although it is obvious that Mrs. Schlemihl has had considerable power in their marriage, *she alone cannot change the rules.* Both partners are required for that, a fact of extreme importance in understanding the interaction in marriage. It takes two to establish the rules.

No partner can singly determine the course of a relationship. The very word "relationship" contradicts this possibility.

72

Rather, the day-to-day interaction of the couple defines, redefines and maintains the permitted behavior of each *vis-a-vis* the other. When a man complains if dinner is not on the table at a particular time and his wife replies with apologies and excuses, this interaction serves to define the relationship and maintain equilibrium between them. If a husband arrives later than usual for dinner and his wife asks for reasons, this too serves to define the relationship, to preserve the roles and rules. In some marriages the husband can eat off his wife's plate in a restaurant but she wouldn't dare take his food without asking. When a husband hands over his paycheck to his wife who earns an equal amount, they are playing by certain implicit rules regarding power and money. Rules are continuously being delineated in a relationship.

Most marital arguments, regardless of the apparent subject matter, are attempts to define the relationship in terms of control: who is "one-up" and who is "one-down." In the Schlemihl story, the domineering wife has invariably been one-up and her husband one-down. Now he is challenging the basic structure of their relationship; they must renegotiate the rules. The ensuing argument in the Schlemihl household (which we can already anticipate) will *seem* to be about whether or not the husband comes out from under the table. The real issue, of course, is who is in control.

The feelings of frustration that follow most arguments are the result of dealing with pseudo-issues—like whether Mr. Schlemihl comes out from under the table, or whose turn it is to feed the dog. Partners argue about facts and deeds; each maintains that he is right and tries to convince the other of this. And strange as it seems, even when one has the facts to prove himself right or the other wrong, these facts often settle nothing. They may provide momentary satisfaction for the one who is "right," but the frustration remains. The basic and pressing question of how these two people *are* in their relationship is left untouched.

When we're getting what we want, we don't worry about who is right or who is in control. Life is good when we feel loved, wanted, and appreciated for just being who we are. But when we don't get the look, the touch, that tells us we're special, then we tend to blame the people closest to us. They are convenient, and they are the ones we want something from. We don't blame them directly for not giving us the tenderness we crave. We substitute complaints that are easier to talk about. So we blame our partner for always wanting his own way. Or we argue about who is acting like a spoiled child, or wanting to be boss. We build cases to prove ourselves right, as if life were being lived out in a court of law. We become experts at explaining, rationalizing, and justifying, as we reply to questions such as, "Why did you do that?" and "Why are you feeling that way?" These questions are easily interpreted as, "Why must you be as you are?" They are like the points surrounding the target. At the bull's eye are the relationship issues: what we want and need from each other.

In our story Mrs. Schlemihl may now use the fact that her husband won't get out from under the table as ammunition against him. How can a woman be married to a man who won't get out from under a table? She can build a case that convinces her and her friends that she is indeed innocent, that her husband is not only stupid but at fault for disrupting their harmonious union. More useful at such a time would be to go beyond defending and blaming and take a look at what is going on. A momentary recess from the game would allow them to observe what is happening between them from a slightly removed position. Even they, the protagonists, might be moved to laughter by their absurdity.

Probably the most destructive pattern in Mr. and Mrs. Schlemihl's story is their blatant use of each other as instruments to fulfill their own needs. Just as the ogre's wife in Chapter II feeds into her husband's tyranny by her attitude and actions, so Mr. Schlemihl plays into his wife's need for absolute control while his wife goes along with his need to be controlled.

In the circular and entangled relationship that is marriage, countless issues come up that establish the rules of being together: who sleeps on which side of the bed, who deals with the money, who decides when to have sex, where to go on vacation, who can criticize whom under what circumstances. These questions have triggered many stormy quarrels.

Decisions are made, issues settled or tabled; sometimes to mutual satisfaction, sometimes leaving a residue of resentments. As resentments grow, or circumstances change in other ways, renegotiation becomes necessary. But some controversies get relegated to the category of "issues already dealt with." Others go to the "too dangerous" category. Eventually, relationship struggles are channeled through topics that are considered "safe."

Mr. Schlemihl makes a dangerous move in disputing his wife's right to be in complete control, especially in front of her friends. It is never easy to lose face. More importantly, he tries to change perhaps the most basic law in their marriage. At the point when he says, "I won't!" he is redefining the relationship—not for all time, perhaps only for the moment, for his wife's response is left to our imagination.

"I'll show you that I'm still master in this house!" is much more than an ironic punch line. This man is telling us something profound. He is saying that in a subtle sense *he* has been the master right along. A master is by definition one who has another subject to his will. From Schlemihl's point of view, this is precisely what he has accomplished. He has successfully manipulated his wife into taking control, allowing him to remain a Schlemihl and to avoid taking responsibility for being a man.

At the same time we must remember that it takes two to define a relationship. She, too, was master, getting what she most wanted: to be in control. So it seems that they were each one a master and each one a slave.

Here is a similar situation from real life, reminding us that such things don't happen only in folktales. This is from the Associated Press in October, 1978:

> Every day for twenty years, Antonio Dos Santos wrote his wife, Rosamunde, a love poem.
>
> But Judge John Latey ruled at a divorce hearing that the Portuguese-born Dos Santos didn't write the poems to celebrate the joys of marriage to his English wife, but because his domineering spouse expected her "mild and gentle" husband to write them.
>
> Dos Santos did so, in the hope his wife would leave him in peace, the judge said.
>
> "She dominated him in every part of their life and everything had to be as she wanted," Latey said. During their marriage she "overpowered" him "and made him her creature."
>
> The judge granted Dos Santos a divorce, saying his wife behaved unreasonably.

We can only wonder what happened after twenty years to change the rules around that household.

In both stories we have examples of the crazy deals that we can get into in our search for wholeness and security. Manipulations between couples take many forms. They are not all played out under the table, but they all depend on feelings that we are inadequate, incapable of making a satisfactory life *for ourselves,* either with this partner or without.

QUESTIONS FOR CHAPTER VII

1. To what do you feel most a slave?

2. Are there issues that are "too dangerous" to deal with in your relationship?

3. What rule, or agreement, do you have with your partner that you think is fair? That you think is unfair?

4. What rule, or agreement, would you like that you don't have now?

5. What has held you back from asking for this?

AWARENESS EXPERIENCES FOR CHAPTER VII

1. Each think of and write down on paper one rule in your relationship dealing with each of the following:

   a) work
   b) spending money
   c) food.

2. Discuss the rules, one at a time, using the following pattern:

   Have you ever talked about this rule?
   Do both of you benefit from this rule?
   Who benefits most?
   Can you remember who initiated this rule? How was this done?

Since each of us has his own experience and his own memory, it is to be expected that you won't completely agree with each other in this discussion. Can you trust that what your partner says is valid for him? Can you accept that you may not totally agree? Do you feel like convincing the other that you are "right"?

If it happens that either person has resentments about any of the rules, continue in the following way.

1. State your resentment clearly and succinctly. Example: I resent that I have to account for the money that I spend, but you don't. *IMPORTANT!* Remember, resentments are *feelings*. They may not seem "fair," or logical; they may not "make sense." Every resentment contains an implicit demand. Demands, also, don't have to be "fair," or logical,

or "make sense." Nor does the partner need to promise to comply with a demand. However, it is important for demands to be stated clearly and directly; otherwise, like resentments, they sneak out.

2. State the demand that is implicit in the resentment. Example: I demand that I not be required to account for the money I spend.

   Strange as it may seem, there is always an appreciation that is connected with a resentment. Sometimes this is difficult to acknowledge, or even to become aware of. Like resentments, appreciations are also feelings; they don't have to be logical. Sometimes we may not even *like* what we *appreciate,* as in the example below.

3. State an appreciation that is connected to the topic of the resentment.

   Example: I appreciate that you earn all the money, and you work hard.

AWARENESS QUESTIONS

Can you hear your partner's resentment?

Can you appreciate his experience, even though it may not be the same as yours?

Can you imagine feeling that way in a similar, or different situation?

Can you hear your partner's resentment without feeling that you must do something about it? And the demand?

CHAPTER VIII

THE CONTRARY WIFE

The Contrary Wife

This farmer was brought up for murder of his wife. Well, after the judge had been talking all afternoon to him the farmer said, "It's about time I was going home to feed. But before I go you'll like to know how it all happened."

And the judge said, "That's what we've been asking you all afternoon."

"Well," the farmer said, "it was this way. My wife was one of them contrary sort. And getting up late one Sunday morning I said, 'We'll not go to church this morning; it's getting a bit late.' "

"And she said, 'Yes, we will go, as we always do. Get yourself finished and we'll go.' "

"So when we set off, I said, 'Shall we go the nearest way?' "

"And she said, 'No. We'll go this other way, as we always do.' "

"So going the way she wanted us to, we had to go across

81

a wooden bridge, and I says to her, 'I'll go first and see if it's safe.' "

"She said, 'No you won't. I'll be going first, as I always do.' "

"And when she got half-way across, the bridge gave way, and she went in. And me thinking she would still be contrary, I ran as hard as I could up the stream. And she was that jolly contrary, she went the other way. And so when I got her out, she was dead. She's been contrary all her life," he said.

Is this farmer stupid? Or is he extremely clever? In effect he is telling the judge that it is not *his* fault that his wife drowned. Expecting that she would be her usual contrary self, when she fell through the bridge he ran upstream to find her. Lo and behold she had gone downstream.

"My wife was one of them contrary sort," the farmer tells the judge. From his story we get the picture: he proposes, she disposes. Her opposition erupts, not from her desire to do or obtain anything in particular, but only from her impulse to triumph at the moment. To exert her will is her primary urge. Does she really want to go to church? Does she care which route they take? She may not know what she wants at all, other than to be in charge, to dominate her husband, to cancel out his wishes at every turn.

Mrs. Contrary's tactic is to wait for her husband to say something, then to contradict him. Nothing that he suggests is acceptable, nothing he does is ever right. Wives like that are impossible to satisfy. If he helps in the kitchen, she shoos him out of her way. If he doesn't help in the kitchen, she complains. If he suggests they go out to dinner, she scolds him for wanting to waste money. If he doesn't take her out to dinner, she nags that they never go anywhere. With her needle-sharp tongue she is always ready to pop his balloon.

The farmer is the perfect counterpart for his contrary wife. He walks into her trap every time. Although he is full of ideas about what they could and should do, his voice is small. In fact it fades to nothing every time Mrs. Contrary opens her mouth.

Was there ever a time when the farmer did take a stand? Did he ever fight back? By the time we meet him he is totally spineless. He takes no responsibility for what they do as a couple, nor for his own actions. He is strictly a "self-defender." Whenever something goes wrong his immediate response is, "I was only doing what my wife told me." Since he makes no decisions, nothing is his fault. Nothing can be blamed on him—not even his wife's death.

And that's how the farmer profits from this relationship with his contrary wife. The farmer can be stupid, or unreasonable, or outrageous, knowing that his wife will always be contrary and pull him back into line. He can stay the way he is; blameless, without a backbone, never taking responsibility for ideas or actions. He can even maneuver his wife, by relying on her opposition, into getting what he wants; for instance, in suggesting that they skip the Sunday church service, he may be seeking to insure that they go.

Do these two remind you of other folktale couples you've met? In reducing their relationship to a rigid, repetitive routine from which they cannot escape, the contrary wife and her husband are very like the ogre and his wife, in reverse, and similar to the fisherman and his wife. Both the fisherman's wife and the contrary wife prevail upon their husbands to do their bidding. The fisherman's wife, however, has far grander aspirations than this simple farmer's wife. She wants to control the world and even the heavens. The contrary wife, like Mrs. Schlemihl, confines herself to controlling her husband.

However, this story has something the others don't have. For the first time, in this folktale, we encounter one partner referring to a long-standing knowledge of the other. We don't hear the ogre's wife say, "My husband has always been a tyrant." Nor does the fisherman remark about his wife's notorious greediness. But here we have the farmer saying that his wife has "been contrary all her life." Either the farmer must have known his wife from the time she was a small child, or she had a reputation in the village, or her parents were outspoken about her contrariness: possibly all three. The important fact is that when he married her, he already had the concept of her being contrary.

When a spouse conceives of his partner as being a particular way—whether it be contrary, brilliant, lazy, or stupid—he often unintentionally encourages or intensifies this characteristic in the other. Just by expecting a certain reaction from the other it will be forthcoming: the self-fulfilling prophecy. The farmer anticipates his wife will be contrary; she is happy to oblige. Then he remarks, "There you go again, being contrary." When she *is* cooperative or accommodating, chances are that he won't comment. He may not even notice; that's not what he's looking for. The farmer can actually lay the groundwork for his wife's contrary reactions: "I don't suppose we ought to try to make it to church this morning." Not only the indecisiveness of the statement, but the shrug that accompanies it and the helpless glance—all beg to be overruled. The farmer is hand in glove with his wife, unwittingly helping to maintain her contrariness.

With their stereotypes of us, others tighten the shackles around us. But what makes this possible are the self concepts with which we have already bound ourselves. "I've always been bossy." "I've always been an unhappy princess." "I've always been contrary." We peg ourselves as a certain kind of person, with certain standards, capabilities, ways of behaving; we tend to live up to our image of ourselves. Our actions "fit" for us. We recognize them and admit to them.

For example, if your self concept includes being a trouble-maker, you can recognize and know yourself when you are behaving so. Your partner may say, "You really cause a lot of trouble around here," and you easily admit, "Yeah, I'm good at that, aren't I?"

Sometimes there is a discrepancy between your picture of yourself and how you actually are. If there's no room in your self image for seeing yourself as a trouble-maker and your partner says, "You really cause a lot of trouble around here," conflict is inevitable. Your denial might sound something like this: "*I* cause a lot of trouble around here! Well, that's a good one. *I'm* the one who is easy going and calm."

We distort and deny. A wife who thinks of herself as completely accepting of her husband, loving and supportive, may not hear how her sly criticisms of him escape. He, however, hears them clearly and responds in anger: "Must you always tell me how to be?" "Who, me?" thinks his wife. "I never tell him how to be." Then she justifies and explains: "I was only making an observation." Or, "I was only stating my opinion." Or, "I was only telling you something I assumed you'd want to know."

Self concepts are self limiting. Through them we reduce ourselves to narrow stereotypes. When we undergo an experience that doesn't fit in with our self concept, we deny and reject the experience and any feelings that might accompany it. In that way we remain strangers to ourselves; meanwhile unacknowledged aspects of our personalities continue to influence us and those around us.

The farmer and his wife are "cardboard" people, limited to habitual patterns that conform to their pictures of themselves and each other. Their responses and habits, once imposed by circumstances they had no control over, have become mechanical, compulsive, and unproductive. They lack awareness.

They don't have to be stuck like that. It's never too late to let some awareness seep in. At any moment it's possible to stop blaming another for ourselves—our intentions, our thoughts, and our actions. This will require expanding the boundaries of our self concepts to include *all* of ourselves—the parts that we shun, deny, and refuse to look at, as well as those that are familiar. No one else can grow for us. That we have to do for ourselves. No one can take responsibility for who we are and what we do. That we have to do for ourselves.

That doesn't mean that we deny the mutuality of a relationship, the interdependence between two people who share their lives. That doesn't mean that when your partner expresses genuine distress, you reply, "That's your problem." That retort suggests that one partner's struggle can be totally separate from his mate's existence—an impossibility. Each partner has his own experience, his own being, his own part, *in relation* to the other. Between the two polarities, "You can't be separate from me, your feelings and actions are my responsibility," and at the other extreme, "You're not going to affect me, nothing you do is related to me," lies an attitude of mutual concern, respect and support.

There is no place for mutual concern among our folktale characters, frozen as they are in their prescribed patterns of interaction. They rely solely on emotional blackmail, shared lunacies, and other manipulations as the basis for dealing with one another. Their automatic responses insure that they remain as they are, inauthentic and out of contact. Like children hiding under the covers afraid of the bogey man in the closet, they are afraid to check out the reality of their fears. They believe the worst. We do the same thing in our relationships. Afraid to expose our fears, we are unable to discriminate between the phantom fears that evaporate in the light of day and those that may be grounded in reality.

Take, for example, a young bride who is in the clutches of her old fears. She prepares breakfast. When her husband makes some comment on her scrambled eggs, she bursts into tears. This can get a marriage off to a bad start: fears, tears, manipulations. Next time her husband has some negative observation to make, however mild, he's going to think twice before he says, "These eggs are runny," or in any way takes issue with her. Most likely he won't say anything about anything! He has fears, too.

If she would only acknowledge her deep-lying fears of falling short of the yardstick of perfection, her husband could probably reassure her that less than perfect is good enough for him, and what's more, the issue happens to be his preference in foods. He likes his scrambled eggs hard.

Consider the situation of a highly paid wife who enjoys a good position. Her less successful husband, unaware of his fear of not being "good enough," lashes out in anger through other grievances, real or imagined. If he could tell his wife how threatened he feels by her successes, she might understand his fears, *without trying to take responsibility for*

87

them. She could show her concern for him and support his efforts to deal with his fear. A constructive alternative to a series of destructive arguments over irrelevant matters!

Joe is a jealous husband. Where does he turn in attempting to change his situation? To himself? Never. To his wife, of course. It's her fault that he's jealous. As long as he thinks that way, argument will follow argument. Closeness and affection will dwindle. Instead, let him turn to *himself.* Let him own and take responsibility for his fear of being abandoned, or of not being lovable. At the same time, his wife can explore what she does to feed his fears, and take responsibility for her actions. This approach may not provide a permanent resolution to their problem, but it opens the way to awareness and personal growth.

"Sure, sure," you may say, "that's easy enough to write about, but that's pretty risky stuff." We all fear that should we experience our feelings of weakness or hostility, we or our partners will not survive. Another bogey man! We're all human. We have all the capacities for feelings and emotions that humans have. When we let go of our concepts and pretenses of how we are, or should be, there's room to experience and develop more of ourselves.

Gradually you can begin to experience yourself; little by little you can allow your long dormant emotions to break free and surface freely. To experience your feelings is to know you're alive. Only now can you express yourself authentically. *If* and *when* and *how* you choose to express yourself is your option. To own your aggression doesn't mean you're going to kill somebody. To own your sense of pleasure doesn't mean you're going to engage in an orgy of unbridled sensuality. On the contrary. Becoming acquainted with and acknowledging your feelings is the first step in having some control over them, rather than being controlled by them.

The contrary wife and her husband obviously never had the courage or the self understanding to get off their merry-go-round of canned behavior. By stubbornly remaining locked away from their own beings—their own essences—they never came alive for themselves or each other.

QUESTIONS FOR CHAPTER VIII

1. What did you want your partner to know about you when you became more than casual acquaintances?

2. Was there something that you *didn't* want your partner to know?

3. What is the "bogey man" in your closet, the fear that you dare not expose to the light of day?

AWARENESS EXPERIENCES FOR CHAPTER VIII

This experience deals with *spite* and *overcompliance*. These are common ways that partners have of withholding, of denying satisfaction to one another. Both of these tactics are ordinarily carried out through actions, but for now, we'll use only words.

1. Sit facing each other. One person (No. 1) tells the other (No. 2) something he would like No. 2 to do, or some way he would like No. 2 to be. This may be something that has been discussed before, or it may be new. It may be of major or minor importance in the relationship.

Example: "I would like you to make meatloaf for dinner some time soon."

No. 2 now answers by telling how he could *spite* the desire of No. 1.

Example: (with enjoyment) "Well, I could tell you that I have already planned something else for dinner for tonight, but tomorrow I'll make meatloaf. Then tomorrow I could forget, and the next day I won't have time, and . . ."

Now reverse the roles so that No. 2 tells something that he would like No. 1 to do, or some way that he would like No. 1 to be. No. 1 answers by telling how he could spite the desire of No. 2; don't forget to enjoy it.

Each take three turns.

2. Now repeat the experience with this difference: rather than spiting the wish of the other, tell how you could *overcomply*. (The wish may be the same as in the first part or different.)

Example: No. 1 says, "I would like you to make meatloaf for dinner some time soon." No. 2 tells how he could overcomply: "Yes, I'll make meatloaf tonight. And when you come to the table tomorrow, you'll see meatloaf again. And guess what you'll have the next day! Why, I could make meatloaf twenty-five days out of every month!

AWARENESS QUESTIONS:

Did you confine your interaction to the instructions?
Could you allow yourself to enjoy the spiting and over-complying?
Did you feel mean?
Talk about how you felt when your partner spited or overcomplied.
As you do this, confine yourself to your feelings and reactions.
Avoid blaming and defending.

CHAPTER IX

GUDBRAND AND HIS WIFE

Gudbrand on the Hillside

There was once upon a time a man whose name was Gudbrand. He had a farm which lay far away up on the side of a hill, and therefore they called him Gudbrand on the Hillside.

He and his wife lived so happily together, and agreed so well, that whatever the man did, the wife thought it so well done that no one could do it better. No matter what he did, she thought it was always the right thing.

They lived on their own farm, and had a hundred dollars at the bottom of their chest and two cows in their cowshed. One day the woman said to Gudbrand:

"I think we ought to go to town with one of the cows and sell it, so that we may have some ready money by us. We are pretty well off, and ought to have a few shillings in our pocket like other people. The hundred dollars in the chest we mustn't touch, but I can't see what we want with more than one cow. It will be much better for us to sell one as I shall then have only one to look after instead of the two I have now to mind and feed."

93

Yes, Gudbrand thought, that was well and sensibly spoken. He took the cow at once and went to town to sell it; but when he got there no one would buy the cow.

"Ah, well!" thought Gudbrand, "I may as well take the cow home again. I know I have both stall and food for it, and the way home is no longer than it was here." So he strolled homeward again with the cow.

When he had got a bit on the way he met a man who had a horse to sell, and Gudbrand thought it was better to have a horse than a cow, and so he changed the cow for a horse.

When he had gone a bit further he met a man who was driving a fat pig before him, and then he thought it would be better to have a fat pig than a horse, and so he changed with the man.

He now went a bit further, and then he met a man with a goat, and, as he thought it was surely better to have a goat than a pig, he changed with the man who had the goat.

Then he went a long way, till he met a man who had a sheep; he changed with him, for he thought it was always better to have a sheep than a goat.

When he had gone a bit farther, he met a man with a goose; and so he changed the sheep for the goose. And when he had gone a long, long way he met a man with a cock; he changed the goose with him, for he thought, "It is surely better to have a cock than a goose."

He walked on till late in the day, when he began to feel hungry. So he sold the cock for sixpence and bought some food for himself.

"For it is always better to keep body and soul together than to have a cock," thought Gudbrand.

94

"He then set off again homeward till he came to his neighbor's farm and there he went in.

"How did you get on in town?" asked the people.

"Oh, only so-so," said the man; "I can't boast of my luck, nor can I grumble at it either." And then he told them how it had gone with him from first to last.

"Well, you'll have a fine reception when you get home to your wife," said the neighbor. "Heaven help you! I should not like to be in your place."

"I think I might have fared much worse," said Gudbrand; "but whether I have fared well or ill, I have such a kind wife that she never says anything, no matter what I do."

"Aye, so you say; but you won't get me to believe it," said the neighbor.

"Shall we have a wager on it?" said Gudbrand. "I have a hundred dollars in my chest at home; will you lay the same?"

So they made the wager and Gudbrand remained there till the evening, when it began to get dark, and then they went together to the farm.

The neighbor was to remain outside the door and listen, while Gudbrand went in to his wife.

"Good evening!" said Gudbrand when he came in.

"Good evening!" said the wife. "Heaven be praised you are back again."

"Yes, here I am!" said the man. And then the wife asked him how he had got on in town.

95

"Oh, so-so," answered Gudbrand; "not much to brag of. When I came to town no one would buy the cow, so I changed it for a horse."

"Oh, I'm so glad of that," said the woman; "we are pretty well off and we ought to drive to church like other people, and when we can afford to keep a horse I don't see why we should not have one. Run out, children, and put the horse in the stable."

"Well, I haven't got the horse after all," said Gudbrand; "for when I had got a bit on the way I changed it for a pig."

"Dear me!" cried the woman, "that's the very thing I should have done myself. I'm so glad of that, for now we can have some bacon in the house and something to offer people when they come to see us. What do we want with a horse? People would only say we had become so grand that we could no longer walk to church. Run out, children, and let the pig in."

"But I haven't got the pig either," said Gudbrand, "for when I got on a bit further on the road I changed it for a milch goat."

"Dear! dear! how well you manage everything!" cried the wife. "When I really come to think of it, what do I want with the pig? People would only say, 'over yonder they eat up everything they have.' No, now I have a goat I can have both milk and cheese and keep the goat into the bargain. Let in the goat, children."

"But I haven't got the goat either," said Gudbrand; "when I got a bit on the way I changed the goat and got a fine sheep for it."

"Well!" shouted the woman, "you do everything just as I should wish it—just as if I had been there myself. What

96

do we want with a goat? I should have to climb up hill and down dale to get it home at night. No, when I have a sheep I can have wool and clothes in the house, and food as well. Run out, children, and let in the sheep.''

"But I haven't got the sheep any longer," said Gudbrand, "for when I had got a bit on the way I changed it for a goose.''

"Well, thank you for that!" said the woman; "and many thanks too! What do I want with a sheep? I have neither wheel nor spindle, and I do not care either to toil and drudge making clothes; we can buy clothes now as before. Now I can have goose-fat, which I have so long been wishing for, and some feathers to stuff that little pillow of mine. Run, children, and let in the goose.''

"Well, I haven't got the goose either," said Gudbrand. "When I got a bit further on the way I changed it for a cock.''

"Well, I don't know how you can think of it all!" cried the woman. "It's just as if I had done it all myself. —A cock! Why, it's just the same as if you'd bought an eight-day clock, for every morning the cock will crow at four, so we can be up in good time. What do we want with a goose? I can't make goose-fat and I can easily fill my pillow with some soft grass. Run, children, and let in the cock.''

"Well, I haven't got a cock either," said Gudbrand. "For when I had got a bit further I became so terribly hungry I had to sell the cock for sixpence and get some food to keep body and soul together.''

"Heaven be praised you did that!" cried the woman. "Whatever you do, you always do the very thing I could have wished. Besides, what did we want with the cock? We are our own masters and can lie as long as we like in the mornings. Heaven be praised! As long as I have got you back again, who manage everything so well, I shall neither want cock, nor goose, nor pig, nor cow."

Gudbrand then opened the door. "Have I won the hundred dollars now?" he asked. And the neighbor was obliged to confess that he had.

We would all agree that Gudbrand makes some unwise decisions, shows a lack of business acumen, and that his wife is a bit silly in her goodness. We might even suspect her authenticity at times. Her constant understanding might drive some men to drink. An unrealistic exaggeration, she is not held up as a model wife. But we must admit they both win at the end.

When Gudbrand arrives home and relates his experiences his wife has every opportunity to confront him with their absurdity. "How could you do such a stupid thing?!" But she doesn't. Instead she identifies with her husband and affirms him by saying, "The very thing I would have done myself." Gudbrand's wife knows something that few of us realize; she does not use marriage as a debating society. It is so difficult for many of us, trained as we are in logical argument, to realize that the art of reasoning and polemics has nothing to do with a relationship or with understanding human behavior. Reason says nothing about getting along with people.

In a marriage we may prove ourselves right to our satisfaction, but in doing so we win a hollow victory. Gudbrand's wife does not need to make herself feel better by making her husband feel worse, or to use her husband's mistakes for ammunition to prove herself cleverer than he. She doesn't have a stake in being right in order to make herself feel more significant. In their drive to always be a winner, marriage partners often tend to forget that *winners are married to losers*. Gudbrand's wife, by not engaging in argument, makes them both winners.

When Gudbrand's wife says, "That's the very thing I should have done myself," she shows an ability to put herself in her husband's shoes, to understand, not in an intellectual way, but to appreciate his experience and feelings at that moment. The recognition of how another feels is true understanding. Because we are all unique, bringing our individual responses to various circumstances, it would be impossible to experience all situations exactly as our partner might. Yet, perhaps we have felt similar reactions on other occasions, or could imagine a situation which would cause just such a reaction in ourselves.

A partner's reaction is a subtle, or not so subtle, influence that operates continually to shape our interactions in relationships. In *The Taming of the Shrew*, Petruchio is obvious as he redoubles his efforts to change his bride's behavior. Frequently, without even being aware of it, we modify our reactions and behavior—even our taste—according to the reactions and behavior of our partner. This is a natural adjustment, a way of getting along with another person whom we care about, with whom we are involved, and from whom we are different. We do not have intentionally to "train" or "change" someone for this to happen.

Mr. Gudbrand has evidently learned that his wife will not put him on the defensive by always demanding explanations. "Why in heaven's name did you do that?" Indeed, he tells his neighbor, "I have such a kind wife that she never says anything, no matter what I do." Her responses do not "make sense" when looked at from a practical, logical point of view. She is expressing herself, responding to the changing situation.

The belief that feelings and experiences must make sense and be consistent is a basic cause of much marital conflict. Although we may try to, we can never argue with someone else's experience. A couple is in bed; the wife says she's freezing. Her husband replies, "How can you be freezing? We have three blankets on and the window is closed." Now it may seem stupid or unreasonable to him that his wife is cold, but the fact is, she feels cold. That's what *is* for her. Or a man takes a sip of coffee at breakfast and says he burned his tongue. His wife says, "How can you burn your tongue? I just drank mine and it's not that hot." In both cases one person denies the other's experience. These incidents may not be critical, but when one partner questions the other's basic emotions, he is denying the other's existence.

"Why" questions such as "Why are you getting mad?" or "Why does that hurt you?" most often are heard as accusations. "You shouldn't get mad." "You shouldn't be hurt." Yet our immediate response to hearing our partner say, "I'm bored," or "I'm feeling depressed," is often the accusing, "Why?" Explanations and justifications follow, an unproductive course that rushes headlong into argument. Sometimes that's just what we want. Embarking on an argument is like scratching an itch. You know you are exacerbating the situation, but oh, it feels so good. Later you are left raw and wondering whether it was worth it.

"Why" is only one of the "fatal four" argument-starters that lurks, ready to jump off the tip of the tongue at any moment. "You always . . ." and "you never . . ." are other champion phrases for blaming. And leading in the field of self-defending, is, "Yes, but . . ."

A duet of blaming and defending is not harmonious music

to live by. Yet it ensnares us like a melody that intrudes into our thoughts long after we have tired of hearing it. To that accompaniment we jump, without awareness, on the carrousel of "You're wrong and I'm right."

Besides the "fatal four" argument starters, couples cut themselves off from each other by:

Analyzing the other's words, actions, or intentions, telling what the other is doing and interpreting *why* he is doing it: "You're doing that because you were toilet trained too early."

Cancelling out what has been said: "You don't mean that," or, "I can't take you seriously."

Judging the other: "You're stupid," or "You're acting like a child."

Making jokes: "You look cute when you get mad," or "My uncle told me any girl who gets hot under the collar gets hot under the covers."

Explaining: overheard in a restaurant—wife to husband, "Every time I make an observation you explain it to me."

And then there are the never-fail conversation stoppers: "You sound just like your father," "You've said all that before," "I can't listen to you if you're so emotional."

Communication, or the lack of it, is a principal source of problems in marriage. Sometimes one partner simply does not want to talk. When one person is unresponsive, communication seems impossible. The one who wants to talk is left totally frustrated; the silent one assumes the position of power. There are several implicit messages in silence. "I don't want to talk to you," is one. If the silent partner cared to use words, he might say, "I feel trapped by your clever use of words," or, "I don't want to get into a fight with you," or, "I want to frustrate you," or "You won't hear me even if I *do* talk to you." Whatever the reasons for his silence, the result is the same: no talking and frustration for the partner, often for the silent one as well.

Communication involves a sender and a receiver. This sounds so simple for two people who speak the same language. What complicates the process is the "double-decker" kind of message that contains both an explicit verbal meaning and an implicit emotional message. In the sampling of conversation stoppers above, we see perfect illustrations of "double-decker" messages. "You sound just like your father." There's a certain tone of voice that goes with those words which conveys a clear, if implicit message. "Your father" is like a symbol. It has all of the emotional load that symbolic words acquire. "We know what a bastard your father was, how unreasonable, tyrannical, mean, bigoted, heartless, and what a miserable life he caused your mother, and I'm not going to let that happen to me." All of that in a tone of voice? Absolutely. "I can't listen to you if you're so emotional." This carries an overpowering emotional load. Spoken in an impassive tone, the speaker assumes a superior stance of control, suggesting that the other person had better be in control before he (the speaker) can listen. He might just as well suggest that the other is a naughty child who must wash the tears from his face before he can expect anyone to pay attention to him.

These common marital practices are cruel, frustrating, and tragic. They are further examples of how easy it is to slip into unproductive ways of interacting that separate partners and lead to hostile and bitter dead ends.

This kind of thing can be avoided when you forget about who is right and who is wrong, who is good and who is bad, who is innocent and who is guilty. For example, Wife:

102

"I'm feeling bored." Husband: "I hear that as criticizing me for not wanting to go out lately. It makes me want to defend myself." Wife: "No, I'm not criticizing you. I know how you've been and it's (your're) O.K." Or, Wife: "Yes, I do feel like blaming you for my boredom." Here we find responses based on feelings, reactions, and expressions of the self. On the other hand, the way to argument is easy: Wife: "I'm bored." Husband (defensively): "We've done lots of things together lately." Wife: "Name one." And on into the argument which may temporarily alleviate her boredom, but leaves an unfinished situation and bad feelings.

When we try to take responsibility for our partner's feelings, we become confused. So often we don't want to hear what our partner is saying because we feel we must *do* something about his feelings. In order to avoid responding to the demand we hear (which may or may not actually be present), to *do* something about our spouse's sadness, or boredom, or desire, we avoid truly *listening* to and *hearing* what is going on with him.

To listen and hear another—that is so essential, and so rare. There are many ways you can busy yourself and *not* hear. You can count the tiles on the floor. You can listen to the radio. You can watch the T.V. or do your fingernails. And there are still other ways. You can rehearse your reply, build your case, stockpile your ammunition, worry about the demand that is coming to do something to, or for, your partner if you *do* hear him. We can always find distractions. Or, if you want to, you can listen—with your ears, with your eyes, with your heart and guts.

What we all want, usually, is simply someone to say, "I hear you. I can appreciate how you feel." When, or if, there is a demand hooked on to your partner's feelings, then that can be dealt with separately, as this is made explicit.

It would be expecting too much to imagine that when one partner has done something unwise, or hurtful, the other could always react with the understanding of Gudbrand's wife. When you are feeling totally accepting, then your reaction will be as spontaneously affirming as hers. But when you are hurt, or disappointed, or angry, then *that* is your response.

There is a subtle but important difference between setting yourself up as judge and jury by saying, "How could you do such a stupid thing!" and responding with, "I'm upset and angry when I hear what you did," or perhaps simply, "I'm furious!" In the second case you allow the other to respond in turn with his feelings, rather than forcing him into the defensive position of the accused. Then true communication begins, bringing vitality and movement like a fresh breeze.

QUESTIONS FOR CHAPTER IX

1. Are there times when you have difficulty *understanding* your partner's point of view? (This does not mean *agreeing with*, or *liking* the other's point of view.)

2. In what area of your life do you feel least understood by your partner?

3. What is your automatic response when you feel attacked?

AWARENESS EXPERIENCES FOR CHAPTER IX

Sex is a subject often not discussed by couples. When you are in bed making love, it seems a bad time to comment. Later, why say something that might start a fight?

This experience is to encourage clear, direct communication.

1. Each of you make a list of five things you would like concerning making love: more of, less of, or different.

2. Without showing each other your list, each take a turn and guess what is on your partner's list.

3. Now exchange lists. If anything is incomplete or unclear, ask your partner to be more specific.

4. When each understands the other's list, talk about how you feel—*not* how you feel about complying—simply how you are as you read the list.

AWARENESS QUESTIONS

1. How did you feel when you handed your list to your partner? Nervous? Ashamed? Shy? Aggressive? Frightened?

2. How were you as you read your partner's list? Interested? Judgmental? Frightened? Amused?

3. Can you imagine complying with your partner's list? What would get in the way of your doing so? What would make it easier for you to comply?

4. Did you put on your list what you really want, or did you censor?

CHAPTER X

RUMPELSTILTSKIN

There was once a miller who was poor, but he had a beautiful daughter. It happened one day that he came to speak to the king, and, to give himself consequence, he told him that he had a daughter who could spin gold out of straw. The king said to the miller, "That is an art that pleases me well; if thy daughter is as clever as you say, bring her to my castle tomorrow, that I may put her to the proof."

Then, the story goes, the king locked the miller's daughter in a room full of straw with a wheel and a spindle and the threat: ". . . if by the early morning thou hast not spun this straw to gold, thou shalt die."

The poor girl, of course, was greatly distressed. Suddenly a little man came in and asked her, "What will you give me if I spin it for you?" She offered her necklace, which the little man took. He spun 'til morning, and when he was through all of the straw had been turned to gold.

The king was astonished, but being "very avaricious" he was not satisfied. He put her into a larger room filled with straw, again threatening her life if she failed her task. The scene of the previous night was repeated. This time she gave the little man her ring.

The third night the room was even larger. This time she had nothing left to give the little man.

"Then you must promise me the first child you have after you are queen," said the little man.

"But who knows whether that will happen?" thought the girl; but as she did not know what else to do in her necessity, she promised the little man what he desired, upon which he began to spin, until all the straw was gold."

When the king found this task completed, he made the miller's pretty daughter his queen.

In a year's time she brought a fine child into the world, and thought no more of the little man; but one day he came suddenly into her room and said, "Now give me what you promised me." Well, the queen wept and begged and the little man took pity on her. He told her that if she could guess his name in three days' time, she could keep her child.

Each day the little man came and the queen guessed every name she could think of. In addition she sent out messengers to collect every name that was used in the kingdom. On the third day a messenger returned with a story. He had come upon a little man in the woods gaily singing this song:

Today I bake, tomorrow I brew;
Today for one, tomorrow for two.
For how can she know, poor royal dame
That Rumpelstiltskin is my name?!

When the queen said his name, the little man was in such

a fury "that he split in two," and that was the end of him.

We are not told whether the king and queen lived happily ever after. We may suppose they were as happy as any king and queen, providing the king never wanted more straw spun into gold. Happily ever after or not, during the period of this story, they both enjoy good fortune, the kind of fortune we expect in fairy tales.

The miller's daughter is a lucky young lady. With the help of Rumpelstiltskin she outwits the king. With the help of the messenger she outwits Rumpelstiltskin. Her father passed her off as possessing a gift she does not have—she can't spin straw into gold. Nevertheless, she not only escapes with her life; she acquires a crown. With magic and a messenger it all works out.

The king, too, is indeed lucky. He gets what he wants—lots of gold. In addition he has a beautiful young wife and a son, who, we hope, will melt his avaricious heart should he ever learn the truth about how he was deceived.

The rest of us, lacking magic and messengers, don't have it so easy. In the eyes of our partners we pass as a successful business man, a liberated woman, a sexy young woman, or an interesting intellectual . . . bearing the implicit promise of spinning a dull life into golden years. Like the king in the story, our partners want to believe in our magic, as we want to believe in theirs. But soon we're found out. We can't make our partners rich, sexy, or successful. We can't give them a life without pain, without frustration. We are neither wizards nor fairy godmothers. In the cold light of morning we are all discovered: we have no magic.

In spite of that fact, we insist on behaving as if we do. Somehow, in some way, at some future time, we tell ourselves, it will all work out—just as it did for the miller's daughter.

In promising her first child to Rumpelstiltskin, she thinks to herself: "Who knows whether it will happen?"

A young woman confesses: "I always knew he wasn't the right man for me, but I wouldn't acknowledge it to myself. I kept thinking it would work out. Now I have to face up to the truth. It hasn't worked out."

A woman who stands taller than most relates her story: "When we met we had this much (gesturing with thumb and forefinger one quarter inch apart) in common. But he was tall and good looking, and I figured the tennis and dancing would take care of themselves later." Unfortunately, they didn't. Neither his tennis nor his dancing improved. And a couple of problems she had conveniently overlooked, his disposition and his drinking problem, got worse. Twenty years and three children later she gave up her dream of making over this man to her image of a husband, and started dealing with reality.

"I knew she didn't want children," admits a man in his forties. "She had already brought up four kids. But I really wanted to have a family, and I figured it would work out some way. Now I know if I want kids I'll have to leave her, and that's hard after these years we've had together."

We all imagine "it will work out somehow." Everything will be all right. Religious differences, color of skin, different values and life goals, interfering in-laws—we brush aside all these potential crisis points. Yet they don't disappear. They turn up, like Rumpelstiltskin, after a year, or five years, or even twenty years, and demand our attention.

The areas of conflict between two people are almost always present from the first hello. We ignore or deny them. Who wants to focus on the trouble spots? It is so tempting to be swept along by romance, and by dreams. Like the Jumblies in Chapter I, we don't want to listen to the warnings of our well-intentioned friends and family, or to the small voice in our own head casting doubts. Magic will take care of everything.

Do we really believe in magic? Just listen to the language we use when we suspect a problem. "It will work out." "Something will happen." "It will take care of itself." This is magic talk. When we use these phrases we sound as if we believe there is a power, a force, a Rumpelstiltskin, that will dissolve our conflicts and dispose of our problems. With these expressions we lull ourselves, and each other, into giving up responsibility for ourselves and our lives. They suggest that *we* don't have to do anything. Some sorcery "out there" will intervene and "make everything all right."

Magic talk is especially favored by couples who have reached a painful impasse. "We've decided to live apart for six months and see what will happen." Or, "We're giving ourselves one more year together to see what will happen." This is a fairy tale mentality. Nothing is magically going "to happen." *We* cause things to happen. We care enough to be present for each other and to create a satisfying relationship, or we don't. But we don't want to accept that. When nothing happens, it's easier to blame a lack of magic than ourselves. We use magic talk: "We tried another six months together, but nothing happened so we're splitting," rather than responsible talk: "We just didn't do anything," or, "We couldn't do anything," or, "We didn't know what to do."

Even more difficult to say is: "We didn't care enough." For when two people have shared their lives for any time, mixed in with indifference and alienation, there is always some caring. There is appreciation mixed up with resentments, happy memories with the bitter ones.

111

A young wife complains that she never sees her husband. "I thought it was wonderful that he was so hard-working and successful. Now I wish he were not so successful." And a husband who abhorred "ambitious" women thought he had found the woman of his dreams, a woman who was easily contented with home and children. After some years he complained that she was dull. Why didn't she get a job or go to school? Traits, once approved of and prized, become objectionable.

There are innumerable examples. The "easy-going" man is soon described as the "lazy husband." The glamorous bride before long is labeled "vain and self-centered." The helpless woman who makes her husband feel capable and important, in time hangs like an albatross around his neck. Ultimately the conflicts surface and scream for attention.

SCENARIO I

King: My dear Queen, I think it's time you spin more straw into gold.

Queen: (Struck with terror) Oh, my lord, I'm afraid that's impossible.

King: Impossible? Certainly not. You've done it before, you'll do it again!

Queen: But I *didn't* do it before. I never could do it, and I'll never be able to.

King: But I don't understand. That's why I married you! Did you lie to me?

Queen: It's not my fault. My father's to blame. *He's* the one who lied to you.

King: (Angrily) I've been bamboozled! And by a no-account miller and his daughter!

Queen: (Crying) You only married me because you love gold. You don't love me and you never have.

King: I knew I shouldn't have married a poor miller's daughter. Guards! Take her away! Off with her head!

* * *

SCENARIO II

King: My dear Queen, I need more gold. There is a room full of straw and a wheel waiting for you.

Queen: Oh, my dear King. There's something I never told you. I didn't spin that straw into gold.

King: What?? You didn't . . . Well, if you didn't do it, who did?

Queen: (Relates the story of how Rumpelstiltskin came to her rescue and how she guessed his name.)

King: (Recovering from shock) Well, if there was one person in the kingdom who could do it, there must be another. Messengers! Go! Comb the land and find a little man who can spin straw into gold. Don't come back 'til you find him!

And so for years the king and queen waited for another Rumpelstiltskin to be found. The queen was in constant dread of being cast out by the king. The king was forever frustrated in his search for the little man with magic.

After twenty years, the king took sick and died. His queen, with great relief, left the kingdom to her son to rule. She took off with her maids-in-waiting to discover what was going on in the world outside the palace walls.

* * *

113

SCENARIO III

The king and queen are watching their young child on his first horse.

Queen: My dear lord, there's something I want to tell you. Do you remember when my father came to you and said I could spin straw into gold?

King: Of course I remember. I will forever be grateful to him and to you.

Queen: But I couldn't. That was just a story my father made up. You know how he is.

King: (Bewildered) I don't understand. Three rooms of straw were spun into gold and you were the only one there— locked in.

Queen: (Relates the story of Rumpelstiltskin.)

King: Oh, my poor dear. What you must have gone through! My knees grow weak when I realize I could have lost you or our son through my greediness. But, (looking fondly at their son) you know, I've changed a lot since those days.

Queen: I've never been sure how you feel about me. And you know, I was afraid you'd want more gold someday, and (with tears) that you'd never forgive me for deceiving you.

King: (taking her hand) Sometimes when I'm angry or frustrated I do blame you for being only a miller's daughter; but you must know that you and our son are more important to me than all the gold in the world.

Queen: I'm so glad to hear you say that. And I feel relieved that I told you. I was afraid, but I just had to take the chance.

King: (with a smile) I'm feeling only a little cheated. Mostly life feels very good to me now. (Dreamily) But it would be nice if you could spin straw into gold.

The king and queen, when left to their own devices rather than relying on outside magic, have the same choices as the rest of us. In the first scenario, they carry on their interchange out of their well-practiced roles. The individuals themselves are lost; blaming and defending assure no contact between them. The king's simple solution: "Off with her head!" corresponds to the present day: "Get yourself a lawyer, because this is it."

In the second scenario, the king, in his eagerness for gold, listens to the queen's story. Yet there is no person-to-person response. Their lives are lived out side by side, but separately. With the king's eyes peeled for a returning messenger and the queen dreading the king, they never come face to face to weave a life together, to create a marriage.

In the third scenario, the queen initiates the dialogue. Her statement includes both herself and the king: "I" and "you." "There's something *I* want to tell *you*." When the king hears her story he responds as one human, capable of experiencing emotions, to another: "What you must have gone through!"

These are not programmed robots; they are people. They have bodies. The queen cries, not as a manipulation but as an expression of her emotions. The king feels weakness in his knees. They touch hands. They experience a variety of emotions and relate these to one another. They are present and able to respond.

Therein lies our own magic.

QUESTIONS FOR CHAPTER X

1. Did your friends or family "warn" you about your mate?

2. Were their warnings well-founded?

3. Had you already "warned" yourself about the same things?

4. When you started your relationship, what did you think would "take care of itself"? Did it?

AWARENESS EXPERIENCES FOR CHAPTER X

Often we are so busy talking, either to ourselves in our heads, or to others, that we cease to experience anything else. During this exercise, allow your perceptions to have first priority. Do this with no talking.

Sit together facing each other. Decide who will go first. This will be No. 1.

Both close their eyes. No. 1, put your hands gently up to your partner's face and explore with your fingers. Feel the texture of the skin, over the eyes, the eyebrows, and slowly all over the face. Feel the structure under the skin: the soft places, the hard places. Feel the air go in and out the nose. Take some minutes; don't hurry.

When No. 1 has done this, No. 2 begins and does the same. Remember, you both have your eyes closed during this experience, and do not talk until you both have done it.

Now talk about this experience with each other. Did you enjoy this? How did you feel?

AWARENESS QUESTIONS:

1. Were you able to stop your inner dialogue some of the time?

2. What surprised you when you were feeling your partner's face? When your partner's hands were on your face?

CHAPTER XI

THE HUSBAND WHO WAS

TO MIND THE HOUSE

This is the story of a man named Fritzl and his wife, Liesi. They lived on a patch of land where Fritzl plowed the ground, sowed the seeds, and hoed the weeds. He cut the hay, raked it, and stacked it in the sun. He worked hard from day to day.

Liesi had the house to clean, the soup to cook, the butter to churn, and the barnyard and the baby to care for. She, also, worked hard from day to day.

But Fritzl always thought he worked harder. When he came home from the fields he sat down, mopped his face with his big, red handkerchief, and complained:

"Hu! How hot it was in the sun today, and how hard I did work. Little do you know, Liesi, what a man's work is like, little do you know! *Your* work now, 'tis nothing at all."

" 'Tis none too easy," said Liesi.

"None too easy!" cried Fritzl. "All you do is putter and

potter around the house a bit—surely there's nothing hard about such things."

"Nay, if you think so," said Liesi, "we'll take it turn and turn about tomorrow. I will do your work, you can do mine. I will go out in the fields and cut the hay, you can stay here at home and putter and potter around. You wish to try it—yes?"

Fritzl thought he would like that well enough—to lie on the grass and keep an eye on his Kinndli-girl, to sit in the cool shade and churn, to fry a bit of sausage and cook a little soup. Ho! that would be easy! Yes, yes, he'd try it.

Well, at dawn Liesi was off to the fields with the scythe on her shoulder, and Fritzl was cooking sausage over the fire in the kitchen. Deciding he needed some cider to go with the sausage, he went down cellar to fill his mug. But he heard a clatter in the kitchen so he ran upstairs—just in time to see the dog flying out the door with the string of sausage. Meanwhile the cider was streaming out of the barrel in the cellar.

Fritzl's day went from bad to worse. His little daughter emptied the butter churn all over herself while Fritzl was putting the cow up on the sod roof to graze. Fearing the cow would fall off the edge, he tied a rope around her neck, dropped the rope down the chimney, and tied the other end firmly around his waist. The cow fell off the roof and Fritzl was whisked halfway up the chimney, where Liesi found him when she returned from the fields.

"Na, na, my man!" said Liesi. "Is that the way you keep house—yes?"

"Oh Liesi, Liesi!" sputtered Fritzl. "You're right—that work of yours, 'tis none too easy."

119

" 'Tis a little hard at first," said Liesi, "but tomorrow, maybe, you'll do better."

"Nay, nay!" cried Fritzl. "Please, please, my Liesi—let me go back to my work in the fields, and never more will I say that my work is harder than yours."

"Well then," said Liesi, "if that's how it is, we surely can live in peace and happiness for ever and ever." And they did.

On the face of it, Liesi and Fritzl have solved their problem. He acknowledges that her work is "none too easy," and returns to the fields, earmarked by tradition as "his" terrain; she marches triumphantly back to the house and to "her" work.

Surely they were not the first, nor the last couple to fight out the "who works harder" controversy. In the everlasting striving between the sexes, that is one of the most common comparisons made. This perpetual competition has us comparing everything from life-expectancy to physical and mental prowess, to intensity of orgasm. To prove what? To prove what Fritzl and Liesi both wanted to establish: "Not only am I important, but I'm more important than you."

The implied boast is: "You need me more than I need you." Historically, this has been more than idle bragging on the man's part. While the woman created the home and cared for her man and their children, it was the man who provided them with the necessities of life. Her existence and that of their children literally depended on his staying with them. The man played first fiddle; he assumed the position of power in the relationship. When he asserted, implicitly or explicitly, "Be nice to me or else you'll be alone, and you can't make it without me," his message fell on acquiescent ears.

A woman may not have given her man the satisfaction of hearing the words, "You're right," but by her actions she made it clear that she believed him. Her habitual response to her man's accusation/threat has been to adapt and accommodate. She marched to his drum, whether it was moving from farm to city, cooking rice instead of potatoes, or watching football games. Husbands have rewarded or punished with money, like the man who, when he discovered his wife had had sex with someone else, took credit cards out of her wallet and cut them to pieces. As long as the paycheck was ensconced in the man's pocket, he held the trump card. His wife had no choice.

Women, of course, have not been completely without power or device for keeping their men. Bearers and tenders of their children, they have used this position skillfully; men want heirs, and want to be around while they are growing up. Women have also made themselves indispensable in the care and feeding of husbands! But their strongest card has been sex. Women have used sex as men have used money—to attract, manipulate, and hold on to their men.

The growth of the women's movement ushered in sweeping changes. The majority of women have their own paycheck in their pocket. Increasingly women raise their voices to influence the decisions that affect them. In the community and at home they are saying in a thousand ways, "I'm important, too."

Whereas women earlier were expected to adapt and accommodate to the needs and desires of men, they now speak of their own needs and desires. Instead of, "Okay, if you want, we'll have a baby," now it's, "Yes, I want a baby, too, but I will not give up my career." And, "I won't be home for dinner tonight; I'm going directly from work to class."

121

"I'm going away for a few days to a workshop for my job."
"No, I don't want to move to another city, even if it means a promotion for you."

The waves created by these major shifts have swept into every corner of society; each household and business is touched to some degree. Traditions are little help as we feel our way, creating, as well as adjusting to, the changes. Women experiment with increased independence, not always with the aplomb of Leisi. While at one end of the scale some few rise to positions of power and top salaries, many others are frustrated in the reality of what has long been a man's world. In boardrooms and bedrooms both men and women have had to reasess their roles.

Men don aprons, and with a far greater measure of expertise than Fritzl, show their skill in the kitchen. Daddy's are in style, diapering the newborn, carrying babies on their backs, and picking children up from school. A couple juggling jobs, children, and household chores is a precarious act. "We're even too tired for sex," is a frequent complaint. The argument of who works harder has not gone out of style, as women discover they still assume the lion's share of household responsibility.

She: "You didn't do the laundry?"
He: "You didn't remind me."

Women wonder at times whether their gains have exacted too high a price. Then, for some, the story of the prince rescuing the damsel and taking her to his castle has a secret attraction. And men, who were not asking for changes in the first place, wonder where they fit in the lives of these busy women; or do they? They are constantly having to learn new norms of behavior, all set, it would seem, by women.

Yet, for the man who is open to the challenge, there are powerful benefits in the new scheme of things. He can watch with pride as his partner succeeds in the world. He can share his life with someone who is excited and happy about her life, someone who takes responsibility for herself. He no longer carries the entire financial burden of the family. His life expands through his mate's activities outside the home; he is not the family's only window to the outside world. And he is released from the rigid male roles that have narrowly defined who "a man" is, and what "a man" does.

The old restrictive, inhibiting definitions of masculine and feminine go hand in hand with power games and manipulations. As we liberate ourselves from traditional roles, the archetypal weapons of both sexes are rendered impotent. So now who is more important?

Nobody. Men and women are equally vulnerable. The social and economic pressures that formerly kept couples together have diminished. When there is no mortar, what binds the bricks? When the lures and bonds which captured and held mates are useless, what is to hold a couple together? As is evidenced by the number of couples who part, when the old necessity of staying together is gone, they are left with nothing.

Today's conditions demand a new kind of mortar. Do we love each other? Are we happy? Can we communicate? Are we friends? Earlier, if couples shared this sense of companionship and love, they were lucky; they had over and above what was expected. But generally the questions didn't even come up. They were man and wife forever. Now we need to have a yes answer to all those questions. Our intimate relationships depend on it. What used to be luxury and trimmings has become the essence.

Love and friendship require contact. We make this kind of contact when we deal with what is really going on between us. Returning to the story of Liesi and Fritzl, we see that they don't have the remotest idea about the struggle in their relationship. Even before the disastrous switch of jobs, Fritzl is clearly in the "one-down" position. He harps on how hard his work is and depreciates Liesi's work. Her confidence, on the other hand, attests to her subtle dominance. "Tis none too easy," she answers him, and calmly challenges him to try minding the house.

Fritzl, in his clumsy way, is asking for appreciation for what he does. He wants assurance that he's important to Liesi. She, in turn, wants the same thing from him. But neither hears the other. Instead of focussing on the process in which they are engaged, they get sidetracked into the apparent content of their argument— who works harder. They miss entirely the opportunity to deal with each other on a significant, personal level.

The ingredient of personal contact in a relationship is like adding yeast when baking bread: what would otherwise be flat and heavy, becomes light, tender and inviting.

QUESTIONS FOR CHAPTER XI

1. Do you tell your partner he is important to you? How?

2. How do you get the message that you are important?

3. Are sex and money trump cards in your relationship? How?

AWARENESS EXPERIENCES FOR CHAPTER XI

This is called a blind, or trust walk. It is done with *no* talking. As in the previous experience, let your perceptions have first priority.

Without words, choose who will be "blind" first. That person closes his eyes. The other person is the guide, and remember, guide, you must watch for the safety of your partner. Take your partner by the arm, or hand, whatever is comfortable, and lead him for about fifteen minutes, providing him with a variety of experiences: moving, smelling, tasting, touching, perhaps meeting other people. Be creative! It is preferable to do this out of doors if possible.

After fifteen minutes switch so that the one who was guide closes his eyes and becomes "blind" while the other opens his eyes and becomes the guide. The new guide leads his partner for about fifteen minutes, also providing a variety of experiences.

When each has had a turn being "blind," talk together about this experience.

AWARENESS QUESTIONS

1. Did you trust your partner when you were blind? Did it take some time to feel trust?

2. Did you tease or play tricks on your partner when you were the guide?

3. Some guides are very protective, holding their partners close and tight. Other guides give their partner much room to move and explore. What kind of guide were you?

4. Did you guide your partner the way you wanted to be guided? Was that how your partner wanted to be guided?

5. Which did you prefer—being guide or being "blind"?

6. Did you learn anything about your relationship from this experience? What can you do with this knowledge?

7. Did you do anything to sabotage this, or any other, awareness experiences? If the answer is "yes", you may find it enjoyable and profitable to go through the series again, being aware this time of any desire or attempt to sabotage you or your partner's involvement.

CHAPTER XII

BEANSTALKS, FOLKTALES, AND GOOD OLD MARRIAGE

Beanstalks that reach above the clouds, and ogres with fortunes in golden eggs exist only in folktales. But in both folktales and real life we find relationships. We find tyrannical husbands and sabotaging wives; we know demanding wives and indulgent husbands like the fisherman and his wife; we meet frightened Titty Mouse and Tatty Mouse, and bold couples like the Jumblies setting off with high hopes. In varying degrees and combinations we all recognize these ancient marriages in our towns and in our own homes. Can attitudes and behaviors ever really change?

Yes, they can. When we learn how to pay attention to them. In this book we have looked closely at marriage relationships, but to find ourselves in these pages is not enough. To transform our marriages into more vital unions is the next necessary and challenging step. For that is where all the potential lies: not in recognizing in a detached way what is happening with a friend's marriage, or even our own, but in risking involvement with ourselves and our partners. *What is the catastrophe in coming alive with your partner?* By daring to experience what we are doing when we create distance as well as when we make contact, we can begin to take responsibility for our behavior and our relationship. *What goes on in our own folktale is our responsibility.*

Are there treasures to be found in marriages? Yes, there are, and they are treasures that, although they exist in degrees in other circumstances, are to be found in their greatest richness through marriage. The very condition of being in relationship, in process with one other person who is most special, is without a doubt a treasure. When this relationship has continuity and stability, as it can in marriage, the treasure increases.

Marriage involves two people who know each other well, possibly as well as they know themselves, or better, and still love one another. They are available to lend support when support is needed; they are present for each other to listen, to care, to sympathize, to laugh at and laugh with. They are there to allow each other just to be, in a non-threatening corner of the world where one doesn't have to play a professional role, or make a living, or prove oneself.

For two people to know each other as well as they know themselves necessitates being with, seeing and hearing one another openly. When we approach our partners openly, although perhaps awkwardly and with uncertainty, we have the exciting prospect in store for us of touching and being touched by another, different from ourselves, of course, yet one fundamentally similar to us. We both have the capacity to experience similar fears and dreams, the same emotions, although perhaps expressed in different ways and to different degrees; we both can hurt, can cry, can love, and laugh; we both wish for acceptance and love.

In a good marriage, one can make a mistake and not lose

130

a friend; marriage survives mistakes. One can express honest thoughts and feelings; marriage transcends momentary anger and misunderstanding. Temporary sentiments of hate and ill-will can be diluted and washed away with the expression of love and concern. When we fall in love with illusions, love disappears when the illusions evaporate. When we love a real person, not only can we accept their being human, but our love can deepen as we experience all facets of their human-ness.

In an enduring marriage we have the chance to see each other in the perspective of time. How rare this is, and precious, for our mobility in the world can take us away from parents and other relatives and childhood friends. And often, parents, relatives and childhood friends don't want us to grow up and become uniquely ourselves. They perhaps have other plans for us. In a marriage we have a growing accumulation of common memories and shared dreams. We can learn to overcome our fears of not being in control of our partner, and trust in each other to be responsible adults, each in charge of his own development and evolution.

The marriage relationship can be the most fertile soil for realizing our potential as human beings. You learn to adapt, to bend, to be more flexible in your lives. You understand the experience of compromise, of overcoming petty biases and irritations. You have the constant opportunity to mature, and the sobering realization that you don't "reach maturity" once and for all, but rather grow towards it over and over again as you experience yourself, take a stand, take responsibility for your feelings, your choices and your actions. You have the opportunity to double what you see and know of the world around you. For you have only your eyes, ears, and feelings, your knowledge and intuition, but by listening

131

to your partner, you can gain a new perspective, another life experience. In this process, you learn what it means to take another person as seriously as you take yourself.

The perspective of time allows a mutual sharing not otherwise possible between two people. A couple acquires their own jokes, symbols, phrases. One couple who recognized their habit of exaggerating coined the phrase "Book of honest truth." When one wanted to check out the truth of the other's statement, he would ask, "Book of honest truth?" Or if one wanted to assure the other of the veracity of a statement, he would add that phrase.

Time helps us to read the needs and desires of our partners and over time we learn ways to respond that are especially appreciated. One weary husband may want his feet massaged when he comes home from work; a wife wants to share the frustration and triumph in her work or profession. One wants to be asked, "How was your day?"; another to be left alone. In marriage there is always the opportunity to share, to share the small everyday incidents and the most important of life's occasions. Having a marriage partner means having someone who is always aware of our existence, someone who knows and cares that we are here on earth, someone who knows if we are sick, or in the hospital, someone who cares deeply when we die. It means having someone rejoice with us in our good fortune and having someone commiserate in our misfortune.

Folktales and marriage have both been around for a long time. In folktales the paths leading to treasures are traditionally beset with dangers. Marriage is no different. My hope is that by posting signs and labeling some of the pitfalls, by calling some of the dragons out of hiding, we can recognize and handle them, douse their fires, or at least diminish them.

Then we can discover our own treasure, different perhaps from everyone else's treasure, different perchance from what we had expected. For our treasure is of our own making. Its substance, its value, its very existence depends on what we invest of ourselves. Unlike the treasure in folktales, the treasure in marriage is not won or lost for all time. Each new day, each new moment, presents us with a fresh opportunity.

EPILOGUE

One of the great uses of literature is to learn more about being human and thus learn more about ourselves, others and the world. We seldom realize that we are creating stories all the time, speaking our narratives to ourselves several times over, and sometimes out loud to others. Some people walk along the street mumbling to themselves, perpetually telling their stories; they are the unfortunate ones who have no one to listen to them. Perhaps they never had. I remember walking home from a girl scout meeting with a friend—two shy ten-year old girls—on an already dark winter afternoon in New Hampshire, and being stopped by a man, drunkenly repeating to us, "I get up in the morning, put on my old pants, and go to work..." Others of us automatically and repetitively recount our tales to strangers sitting beside us on an airplane, or friends and relatives who are too polite to remind us they have heard it all before. These narratives we tell are based on anecdotes from our experiences: the fine times, the hard times, the everyday situations, descriptions of ourselves as heroes and as victims. Our stories become the bases for our future experiences as we reproduce them not only in our thoughts but on our outer stage as well, bringing in real people to play the supporting cast to our own central role. So we tell our story and create our story both at the same time. Unfortunately, we can get stuck, stagnate in boggy places, self-hypnotized in powerless roles that we play out over and over again in a living death. Like the folktales, our stories persist.

There are books for children in which the reader is instructed where and when to insert the child's name. Here is an adventure where the child is the main character! What could be more engaging for a youngster—or an adult? Isn't that what we do when we read a book or see a film? We enter in to the narrative. *We* have the adventure. This is exactly what can occur in Gestalt therapy. We *are* the actor, in the event, here and now, experiencing, exploring and perhaps doing something we haven't done before; this is our story taking its course. Owing to this process, in this place, in this moment, our narrative is of our making—or remaking—coming about through our self-expression, originality, and vitality. And like all good literature, by using a Gestalt perspective, we can create not just one reality, not one single truth, not only one point of view, but perhaps several. It is possible to tolerate paradoxes, holding with awareness opposites within our being. The Gestalt therapist is the listener and witness to the clients' narratives; but more, she or he is a participant through the ongoing relationship which exists between therapist and client.

A principle of Gestalt therapy is to make what is implicit, explicit. I am following this principle now, regarding the text of this book. Although never mentioned specifically, the book is saturated with a Gestalt theory foundation. It is the frame through which I see, hear, and understand behavior. It is the structure I use to explain human phenomena.

The roots of Gestalt therapy go deep and reflect a world view that is systemic, not linear; holistic, not atomistic—the whole is more than and different from the sum of the parts; qualitative, not quantitative; in which knowledge is gained through relationship and in context, through present-centered awareness, not detached observation or analysis of parts; in which process and actuality are emphasized, rather than static abstractions. Although Frederick Perls is generally considered the main developer of the approach, in the preface to the first edition of his earliest book, *Ego, Hunger, and Aggression*, published in 1947, Perls wrote, "In writing this book I have had much help...above all from my wife, Dr. Lore Perls." Here one can find the beginnings of Gestalt therapy, "the perspective," as Perls referred to it in his introduction to the 1966 publication of the book.[1] It has been further developed by Fritz and Laura (Lore) Perls and others over the last half century. In this first book he made "the attempt to reinforce the structure of the psycho-analytical system where its incompleteness and even faultiness is most obvious:

    (a)   In the treatment of psychological facts as if they existed isolated from the organism.

    (b)   In the use of the linear association-psychology as the basis for a four-dimensional system.

    (c)   In the neglect of the phenomenon of differentiation" (Perls, 1969, p. 13).

His fundamental changes were the following: to

    (a)   "replace the psychological by an organismic concept,

    (b)   replace association-psychology by gestalt psychology,

---

[1] Published by Orbit Graphic Arts, San Francisco in cooperation with The Esalen Institute, 1966.

(c)   apply differential thinking based on S. F.
       Friedlaender's 'Creative Indifference'" (Perls,
       1969, p. 14).[2]

Here we see the skeleton which furnished the perspective of Gestalt therapy.

In Gestalt practice, which derives from the above constructs, the encounter is an important source of energy and integration. When a client speaks, she or he is always encouraged to speak *to* some one or some entity. Sometimes this "other" is a character from his or her life story. For example, a client says, "My problems really began when I was four years old and my father left. He left for good. And he never said good-bye." In order to facilitate actualizing the client's engagement and help create a healing experience by supplying what has been missing— incomplete in the life situation—the therapist might suggest that the client tell her or his father directly this same sentence. Father is not really there but it doesn't matter. The imagination of the client is sufficient along with assurance and perhaps modeling by the therapist. (If the client is hesitant this becomes the focus of the work and leads to other types of exploration.) Then a meeting is possible, between the client and the father; not the real father but the introjected father that the client carries within through life. Thus the narrative becomes a drama with an encounter between the two characters, client and

---

[2] Chapter 1 of *Ego, Hunger, and Aggression* presents an exposition of Perls' foundational thinking in the early 1940's. He makes some surprising observations on topics still timely; for example, the impossibility of "objective" science, the failure of cause-effect thinking, and the relationship of the observer and the observed.

137

father. The direct encounter helps to heighten the intensity of the process, thereby involving the totality of the individual: thoughts, (the intellect), words, (speaking), physical expression (the body) and emotions. The scene is set for a possible completion of an unfinished situation from the past. The client's narrative becomes more complete. The relationship between client and the internalized father is altered; the relationship between the client and herself or himself becomes more whole as missing pieces are integrated.

The "other" may also be an unintegrated, or disowned, aspect of the client, with no apparent connection to another person. In the following illustration the source could be an older brother or neighbor from childhood which will become clear during the work. A client says, "There is a part of me that I would love to get rid of: that's the bully in me." There is no actual bully inside the client. What the client is saying is this: in some situations he acts like a bully. He does not like his behavior at those times and he would like to stop behaving that way. "The bully" has become an entity with a life of its own, having the power to do something the client does not like. In this case an encounter between the client and "the bully" would be worth exploring, an opportunity to "exorcise" the powerful introjection which seems to have a life of its own.

A meeting between the "outer" person and the "inner" person is another encounter with potential for discovering life energy caught in an undiscovered story. The possibilities for encounter are unlimited. The "other" can be anyone or anything on which a person projects power. For example, "I have a nightmare that frightens me again and again." Or, "A wall comes up and separates us." The nightmare ,and the wall represent projected power victimizing the client. The above are all examples of fragmentation with accompanying opportunities to move toward further integration, growth, and wholeness.

Gestalt-type interventions have been found effective and have been borrowed by many therapists from other disciplines. Unfortunately, there is often a lack of understanding of the most basic premises, the "skeleton" of the Gestalt approach. An example is the holistic outlook. It is not easy to relinquish the linear conception; it requires a major shift to understand that one partner's behavior is not a cause of the other's behavior. Causes are neither simple nor singular. The behavior of each partner is a *function* of the other's behavior; a function that is complex and non-linear. Partners may, however, induce one another's behavior, or influence it, as when one assumes a dominant and the other a submissive position. In any event, the pair form a system and are part of larger systems, depending where one draws the boundaries. The holistic view includes the relation of an individual to her or his "field," the entire environment over time as well as at any actual moment.

The two-chair dialogue is an illustration of another intervention that has been widely borrowed. It is found beneficial in slowing down and making explicit the sub-vocal conversations we have with ourselves or others. It is useful in bringing out in the open conflicts within an individual, resentments from our past, or with the death of a loved one, to give just three instances. It is not an end point of therapy but rather a part of a larger process of integration work. Therapists might make use of the two-

139

chair dialogue sensitively and to good outcome without an appreciation of the deeper process of reowning projections and being more available for contact, both with oneself and with others. They may be ignorant of the principles of organismic regulation, creative indifference, and holism. When therapists do comprehend the potential power of these principles the effectiveness of their work may well be enhanced with original and creative interventions, tailor made for the occasion.

Gestalt therapy has set a precedence for a flexible, open system to examine and deal with reality rather than an elaborate, codified theory. "Figuring out," which is primarily a cognitive activity, is renounced in favor of experiencing. Explanations, rationalizations, and justifications of our and others' behavior are put aside in favor of contactful interaction. Gestalt interventions of all varieties are meant to be experiments and explorations, whether working with opposites, or interruptions, automatic behaviors or tone of voice; they provide both the client and therapist moment-by-moment information on how the client organizes her or his data. They elicit experiences in awareness and contact.

A vital aspect of all Gestalt work is to maintain a holistic approach; a reminder that our verbal capacities are limited in their use in gaining knowledge of ourselves and others. Throughout work with individuals (as well as couples) it is therefore important for clients to be aware of physical feelings and emotions. These provide a direct route to awareness and self-expression, bypassing reasons "why," explanations of the other's behavior, and all the learned responses we repeat endlessly in our chronicles. Usually our automatic explications have little or nothing to do with what is actually experienced at the moment.

Each response of the client helps determine the facilitator's next intervention. This proceeds step by step toward an unknown outcome. Through such sequences, including meaningful relating between therapist and client, unfinished situations in the client's psychobiography are revealed. Missing aspects of the client's existence are uncovered. Most important in the therapeutic situation is to help secure a foundation for clients for the expansion of their total being. This would encompass deepening and broadening their consciousness, giving importance and meaning to behavior, and extending their present-centeredness for more awareness and contact with themselves and others.

During the last dozen or so years, ways of using personal narratives in psychotherapy have been developed, largely by White and Epston (1990). They share some of the world view of Gestalt therapy, including the importance of personal experience in the present in relation to meaning given to past experiences, the importance of narrative as examples of events developing over time, the appreciation of multiple meanings. Their practice of externalizing and personifying the problem bears resemblance to making what is implicit, explicit, in Gestalt language. They emphasize the client's responsibility for creating his or her narrative and the potential that exists for each person to change their narrative and become the agent in his or her life.

The Gestalt approach maintains a focus on awareness as a primary concern. Because we are so invested—so emotionally involved—in our relationships it is difficult for us to be neutral observers of ourselves and our partner. We might expect scientists to be able to look at phenomena in an unemotional way, yet even they find it difficult, or impossible. Many years ago I read the following quotation attributed to Jack Eddy of the Harvard-Smithsonian Center for Astrophysics: "But the importance of the sun as the ultimate source of energy and life on earth makes it hard to study in a detached way. We demand things of the sun that we don't of other stars." What a surprising example of human fallibility in this statement. With the demands that we put on ourselves and our partners, it is no wonder we cannot take a look at ourselves and our relationships in a detached way. That is where the folktale marriages can come to our rescue.

We can see the interrelatedness of the couples portrayed in folktales. Their stories are our stories—with a difference. We are not threatened by their predicaments as we are by our own; we are not emotionally invested. We can identify with them enough to acknowledge the similarities but not enough to become caught in their systems, as we are in our own. They provide a pleasurable and safe path into our own stories. We might also realize how much we have to work with compared to the astonishing lack of knowledge and skills of the folktale characters. They don't have much fun. Not a sense of humor among the lot. Although what they do together, over and over, doesn't seem to pay off , they never step back and take a look at themselves.

I used the folktale narratives as a vehicle for presenting my outlook on relationships and the pitfalls inherent in marriage. As I stated earlier, it is the frame through which

I look to make sense of peoples' behavior and interaction. I write in Chapter One about becoming entrapped in a net of "shoulds" by wanting to live up to unreasonable standards of an "ideal marriage," and the inevitable failure and the disappointment that is bound to follow. Often we seem to work against ourselves with the same force we exert to achieve our goals. To think about and plan how we should be in the future ("tomorrow" or "from now on"), and confine ourselves to abstractions, generally doesn't succeed. The Gestalt approach sees change as an outcome of awareness and growth through experience, not the result of a vague decision for "self-improvement" or an "ideal marriage." Our attitude and our concrete behavior in the moment is what leads to the creation of a new event. For example, at a particular moment of actual relating, do we let go of our negative judgments, become aware of our actions, and choose to be *with* our partner? Are we *in this moment* helping to create the kind of relationship we say we want? Are we caring, understanding, supporting, keeping a light touch, or whatever the situation calls for, to make positive contact—now? Can we do this with *no expectations*? Ah, this is difficult. When we have expectations and a desired outcome regarding how our partner should be, how he or she should respond, then we begin to manipulate our partner and the situation. We create then what Buber (1970) referred to as an "I-it" relationship. This may work to get what we want in an isolated incident but not in the long run. It will not help to foster a trusting relationship based on mutual respect. Through Gestalt process we continually model and promote availability and responsibility, laying the foundation for an "I-Thou" relationship (to use Buber's term), without our resentments from the past or fears for the future getting in the way.

The above illustrates the difference between goal and process. It exemplifies awareness, choice, and engagement—all ingredients of personal responsibility, of self- actualization in an interaction: meeting, encounter and contact. These themes are reflected in the questions and awareness experiences at the ends of the chapters.

In Chapter Two, I introduce the limited repertoire of the ogre and his wife. Like all couples they have their ways of handling one another. The ogre, the tyrannical husband, "shouts orders and roars his threats." His woman "plays the submissive wife" and "soothes him with her tranquil words." She also lets Jack in the house and becomes his accomplice in crime against the ogre by hiding him in the oven. In Gestalt language, this marriage consists of playing out their roles as "top-dog" and "under-dog." When this type of conflict is carried on within a person, that is, an inner dialogue in which one inner voice makes demands ("Don't eat any more chocolate!") and another makes excuses for not meeting the demands, ("But it's my birthday") it can be a life-long struggle with no rest from a dialogue which is as old as childhood. When one of a couple assumes the top-dog stance in relation to the under-dog stance of the spouse, it will resemble the ogre and his wife in real life, with repetitive demands and acts of sabotage.

Titty Mouse and Tatty Mouse, the couple in Chapter Three, do everything the same. You can't tell one from the other. Do they know about contact? Perls defined contact as "appreciation of differences." This means when one is in contact with another, each has a sense of himself or herself

144

and awareness of the other as a different entity. One's physical sensations, thoughts and emotions are recognized as one's own and different from the other. When no difference is experienced, this is referred to as *confluence* in Gestalt. People in the early stages of romance are delighted with confluence. Each agreement, each interest in common is to be celebrated. For some couples this is the path of least resistance; as time passes it seems easier than carving out a place for oneself, meeting arguments, perhaps, or snide comments about one's choices. "If you loved me you would always agree with me."

The fisherman and his wife represent most couples in one respect: they have their unspoken contractual agreements. Neither partner can possibly be satisfied with their barren existence. Together they live out their life sentences, not imposed by any court of law; solely by themselves. The questions and experiences at the end of Chapter Four provide a good place to start for couples like Mr. and Mrs. Fisherman; they need to talk to each other and become acquainted in new ways. Self-disclosure, that is, talking about one's hopes, dreams, and fears is such a good way to learn about one another. The very process of sharing themselves is often enough to give hope that something could be different. If people have never developed the capacity to be interested in another's story or to listen with empathy, then the initial work might be to grieve for their early years when no one ever listened to them.

The story, The Half-Cup of Tea, always evokes laughter from an audience. Could it be that many of us have had similar experiences? How quickly our pseudo-logical minds leap from, if A is so, then B must be so. If she pours a half cup of tea, she'll be a wonder. If he finds me attractive, he'll be a perfect husband.

In the awareness experiences at the end of that chapter I ask whether readers saw what they wanted to see when they met one another. This brings up the question of our subjectivity and how selective we are in what we see and hear. We are confronted with so much data in simply meeting a person and hearing their voice and words that we could never register all of it. What do we then elect to see and hear from this abundance of information? The culling process is unconscious. We do not say to ourselves, I will only see or hear this and not that. Like the proverbial seven blind men and the elephant, we think what we see, hear, or feel is all there is. Our interests help to dictate what we observe; our attitudes, our needs and desires; our prejudices and our fears. All these and more mysterious impulses—biological and psychological—lead us to see people and respond with indifference or see them as desirable matrimonial material. We take in but a tiny bit of somebody and create the rest from our own self. We project out on to the other what we want to see there and thereupon fall in love. Our friends and relatives can tell us about the bit they see, but are we interested? Of course not. And we set out like the Jumblies in Chapter One, not only in an unworthy craft, but with a stranger as a partner, as inexperienced as we are ourselves. And no compass!

Having mentioned projection in the sense of imagining that another person embodies certain qualities, talents, or attitudes that make them attractive to us, I think it is also important to consider negative projection. On the basis of very little information we can imagine that others personify qualities and characteristics which we consider negative. In either case, whether negative or positive, projection interferes with good contact between people. Rather than responding to the actual person, we look for and see what we anticipate. We are inclined to select those behaviors that reinforce what we "know" about the other and disregard anything that might contradict our bias. Especially with partners, parents and our children we do this. In keeping with the holistic notion that is intrinsic to the Gestalt approach, becoming acquainted with and integrating—or reowning—projections is an important aspect of the therapeutic experience. Working through dreams is considered an effective way of meeting, experiencing, and beginning integration of disowned aspects of the person. Setting up two-chair dialogues, in which one chair is considered the "projection chair," is also a practical and potent way for clients to experience projected attitudes, qualities and characteristics. When seated in the projection chair, clients are provided the opportunity to generate the power they have projected onto a person (or entity) with whom they have chronic conflict, or perhaps an isolated altercation. Clients may discover their own way of expressing power in that chair. It is also possible that they do not have the confidence to express themselves, even in the safety of the therapy session. If, for example, the fisherman imagined his wife sitting opposite him, could he speak up? Could he make demands? When sitting on the projection chair in the role of his wife, he might discover that he has the potential to be his own person, to speak up, make demands, say "no" as well as "yes, dear, whatever you

147

want," at first in the persona of his wife, and eventually as himself.

Growing together takes time and shared experiences, whether they be the birth of a child, the death of a parent, exciting adventures in the out-of-doors, or meeting important challenges. Every day there are chances for intimate moments of sharing, talking, and touching. In this way Gestalt may be considered an "optimistic" therapy; there is always a fresh moment available. Every day there are opportunities for a smile, an appreciation, a reaching out to give or to receive.

What interferes with growing together? We see examples in the folktales: repetitive interactions, no dialogue, no initiative to try out new ways of being, except for Schlemihl in "The Master," and he has a tough job ahead. Fritzl and his wife Liesi did do something different. Tired of hearing him boast about how hard he worked, at the same time belittling her contribution, Liesi donned the overalls and went out to cut the hay. And they, we are told, lived in peace and happiness forever and ever. How fortunate for us that we are not stuck in folktales, except those of our own making. And certainly, if we don't like our stories we can do something different. We can experience the need to change what we have, mobilize energy, and together become engaged in creating and enjoying our narrative as we recreate it, discovering what we want and need along the way.

REFERENCES

Buber, M. 1970. <u>I and Thou</u>. New York: Charles Scribner's Sons.

Perls, F. S., 1969. <u>Ego, Hunger and Aggression</u>. New York: Random House.

White, M. and Epston, D., 1990. <u>Narrative Means to Therapeutic Ends</u>. New York: W.W. Norton & Company.